In praise of Creating Blue Space...

*There is no organization that I admire more, or have learned more from, than R-Arc...the wisdom you gain from **Creating Blue Space** will enable you to change the course of your organization, the lives of the people you support and your own worldview.*

Fredda Rosen, Executive Director
Job Path NYC

*Organizations and agencies looking to transform their existing services to more innovative, individualized supports will find a fantastically helpful guide in "**Creating Blue Space**". Powerful exercises and reflections in the book will improve and change how people help individuals with developmental disabilities to have exceptional lives in the community.*

Ann Hardiman, Executive Director
New York State Association of Residential and Community Agencies

Creating Blue Space *is Meissner's offering to transformational leaders everywhere who are concerned about blazing a trail through an era of uncertainty. This book is a powerhouse combination of advanced organization theory, personal account experience and applied learning opportunity rolled into one remarkable field guide. This is a must-have resource for anyone invested in changing the landscape with and on behalf of people who experience life through disability.*

Carol Blessing, Faculty
Employment & Disability Institute ILR School Cornell University

Creating Blue Space *shows us the crucial importance of following the path less traveled...*

Janice Fitzgerald, Executive Director
Parent to Parent of New York State

Creating Blue Spaces is a beautifully written, ground breaking book. It offers profound thinking about how service agencies, systems, and professionally organized efforts can authentically value and build the gifts and capacities of people on the margin. It makes the connection between the importance of an authentic internal culture and the "good form" we wish bring into our communities in our wish to reduce human suffering. It is one example of how systems can possibly deliver authentic care. While focused on the developmentally disabled world, the wisdom on leadership, conversation, practices and learning applies to all efforts to restore humanity to organizational life. The book is the calm, clear eye at the center of the storm of modernism.

Peter Block, Author and
Partner in Designed Learning

In a public policy world that increasingly seeks to commoditize people who have intellectual and/or developmental disabilities, Meissner stands among the few turning the discussion back to the people who seek support and their rights to true citizenship. In Blue Space Hanns Meissner translates his years of study, commitment and deep organizational change at his agency into a remarkably readable guide for organizations who seek this journey.

Max E Chmura, Human Service Consultant
former New York State Commissioner of the
Office of Persons with Developmental Disabilities

Creating Blue Space

**Fostering Innovative Support Practices
For People with Developmental Disabilities**

Hanns Meissner

INCLUSION PRESS

Library and Archives Canada Cataloguing in Publication

Meissner, Hanns, 1952-, author
    Creating blue space : fostering innovative support practices for people with developmental disabilities / Hanns Meissner.

Includes bibliographical references.
ISBN 978-1-927771-02-0 (pbk.)

    1. Arc of Rensselaer County. 2. Developmentally disabled--Institutional care--New York (State)--Rensselaer County.
3. Developmentally disabled--Services for--New York (State)--Rensselaer County. I. Title.

HV1570.5.U62R46 2013   362.1968   C2013-903154-5

Published by Inclusion Press
Copyright © 2013 Inclusion Press and Hanns Meissner

Printed in Canada by Couto Printing & Publishing
Printed on stock containing post consumer recycled content

Images incorporating Theory U and levels of listening, responding and innovating are modified from materials licensed under Creative Commons by Otto Scharmer and The Presencing Institute, www.presencinginstitute.com/permissions.

Cover design and illustrations by Caits Meissner (http://caits.mvmt.com) on page 17, page 75, page 76, page 78, page 88, page 104, page 147, page 161.

John O'Brien made the rest of the illustrations and tables.

Cover photo by Hanns Meissner

The Arc of Rensselaer County Foundation Board provided financial support to the production and distribution of this book.

INCLUSION PRESS

47 Indian Trail, Toronto
Ontario Canada M6R 1Z8
p. 416.658.5363 f. 416.658.5067
inclusionpress@inclusion.com

inclusion.com   BOOKS ·WORKSHOPS · MEDIA · RESOURCES

In the eye of a hurricane the sky is blue and birds can fly there without suffering harm. The eye of the hurricane is in the very middle of destructive power, and that power is always near, surrounding that blue beauty and threatening to invade it . . .

In a world of moral hurricanes some people can and do carve out rather large ethical spaces. In a natural world and a social world swirling in cruelty and love, we can make room. We who are not pure ethical beings can push away the choking circle of brute force that is around and within us. We may not be able to push it far away, but when we have made as much room as we can, we may know a blue peace that the storm does not know.[1]

—Philip Halle

4

Contents

A word about terminology

Throughout this book I repeatedly refer to The Arc of Rensselaer County (R-Arc), people, persons or individuals with developmental disabilities (individuals, people, persons), and the developmental disabilities field (DD). To eliminate a redundant and cumbersome presentation, I will, at times, substitute the abbreviated forms.

There is a **Glossary,** beginning on page 191, for those who may be unfamiliar with key terms from organizational theory, organization development practice or policy affecting developmental disability services in the US and New York State. Many Glossary entries provide links to more information.

Acknowledgments and Inspirations

This is the story of the individuals, families, and staff who have touched The Arc of Rensselaer County (R-Arc) over the years. This story would not exist without Henrietta Messier, who I single out as the core guide of R- Arc's story. I must acknowledge R-Arc board members and The Arc of Rensselaer Foundation Board past and present for the unwavering support they have given me over the years and the partnership we have in realizing pieces of our ambitious vision. I also appreciate the contributions of the people with whom I closely partner in our operational, tactical and strategic tasks. This work has been made both meaningful and enjoyable by the R- Arc Administrative Team—Jim Blessing, Alisa Hobb, Diane Heaphy, CJ Heins, Tracey Hempel, Chris Liuzzo, Ed Martin, Don Mullin, and Sandy Van Eck—who all share a common vision, values, and sense of humor.

Readers and editors have vastly improved this book. Roger Mitchell, Bert Stern, Jim Blessing, Carol Blessing, Jack Pealer, Max Neil, Oliver Koenig, Pam Walker, Tim Vogt, Steven Muller, Caitlin Meissner, Lindsay Meissner, and my wife Linda Munro have spent countless hours reading drafts of this book and making suggestions for improvements. I owe much to John O'Brien for his substantial edits, page layouts, table design, and ongoing guidance as the book progressed into good form.

Thanks to Caitlin Meissner for her graphic design work throughout the book and on the cover. And to Lindsay Meissner for her substantial final edit.

I appreciate the opportunity that Ann Hardiman and NYSACRA gave me to try out many of the concepts and exercises in sessions of the Individualized Supports Learning Institute.

I acknowledge what I have learned, and put into practice, from organizational thought leaders: Nancy Howes, Don Klein, Chris Arygis, Edgar Schein, Peter Block, Peter Senge, and Otto Scharmer.

An equally significant influence is Joseph Campbell and his insight into the power of myth in formulating meaning in cultures and peoples across the planet. Thanks to him, the use of metaphors in this book helps express meanings that transcend the written words on the page. All the ways that services are designed and implemented are ultimately shaped by the images we often implicitly have in our heads about people with developmental disabilities. These images function as unconscious lenses through which we view our world, determine how we act, and when surfaced reveal our hidden belief systems and assumptions. Therefore, I use metaphors throughout this book as a way to surface beliefs behind our actions, disrupt and shift perspectives, explain various change processes and practices, and hopefully unleash creativity to achieve citizenship for all people with difference.

Friends and Mentors

The encouragement and support I have received from my wife Linda, and daughters Caitlin and Lindsay, has been overwhelming; they are on this journey with me.

Last, I want to recognize the contributions of John O'Brien and Beth Mount for their thoughts and practices, as they are the link from my organization development work to the field of developmental disabilities. They have been mentors, friends, and partners in evolving our supports for people we care about.

Hanns Meissner serves as the Chief Executive Officer of The Arc of Rensselaer County in Troy, New York. Since 1979, he has worked to promote the inclusion of persons with disabilities in all aspects of community life. Holding a Ph.D. in Organization Development from Union Institute, Meissner has consulted with many organizations in strategic management, organization development, leadership and team development, and person centered approaches. Additionally, Meissner was an Academic Director and Associate Professor with Antioch Graduate School in the Department of Organization and Management for over 17 years. Meissner is married with two grown daughters and is an avid hiker and music lover.

For further Information about the application of the concepts, frameworks and exercises contained in this book, contact:

Hanns Meissner

308 Shaver Road

West Sand Lake, New York 12196

518-274-3110 ext. 3021 (work)

518-674-5642 (home)

hmeissner@renarc.org (work)

hannsm@verizon.net (home)

Foreword

People who sense the gap between the reasonable aspirations of people with developmental disabilities and the services typically available to them often choose the word "transformation" to name the change necessary. This suggests efforts that result in a dramatic difference in form and character. Presentations about transformation often invoke the image of caterpillars emerging as butterflies to depict the process and its result.

This book brings substance and weight to the idea of transformation. It tells the story so far of The Arc of Rensselaer County's (R-Arc) generation-long journey toward an organization that is well formed to support people with developmental disabilities to take their rightful place as contributing citizens of their communities. As early efforts succeeded, people discovered new capacities and possibilities. This disrupted R-Arc's sense of what good form for assistance is. Far more people are in good jobs in community workplaces and living securely in their own homes than the designers of R-Arc's day centers and group homes had imagined possible. If people are not to be trapped in buildings built on assumptions proven wrong by the way others are now living, deep change is necessary not just in relationships, practices and settings, but in the very way of making change.

This book is a story of people dealing with one of the most important adaptive challenges facing our field: how to reshape an organization with major investments in serving people in groups in a way that respects the diverse interests and beliefs of the people and families involved while maintaining viability and legitimacy in a service system caged by competing commitments. The story is told from an insider's perspective, by a traveler who has shared responsibility for guiding R-Arc's journey into new paths.

There are books that present transformation as a simple matter of having the courage and persistence to follow the well-marked map laid out within their covers. This is not one of them. There are books that claim attention because they are stories of unmitigated success. The journey recounted here is far from over: the book owns up to the facts that many people are still served as one of a group and individual supports are far from perfect. There are books that pride themselves on being easy to read. You will probably not find this book to be one of them. There are three reasons for these challenges to the reader, and I think they make the book worth the study it demands.

The first is the most important. The transformation of an organization that 185 people rely on for assistance in their home life and about

300 people count on for support with their daily occupation is a complex human undertaking that depends fundamentally on the integrity, commitment and trustworthiness of the relationships among all of the people involved. It is both a matter of discovering and implementing effective practices and an up-close, emotional process that respects the real losses people encounter and the differing estimates of the balance of hope and fear that people sense in change. And, as of yet there is no indication of a final steady state the organization will reach. There may be periods of stability in individual lives, but there is plenty of unexplored territory and much that will be found there will disrupt today's best approximation of good support. This is especially likely to be true for people who require highly skilled support on a continual basis. A rational list of strategic tasks has its uses, but quickly reaches its limit when it comes to matters that people experience as shifting the ground beneath their feet. From the caterpillar's point of view, transformation is daunting, no matter how beautiful the butterfly she will become.

The second reason the book repays study is that transformation demands social innovation. This is the fundamental difference between previous offerings and a good form for the support of valued social roles. Past services offered a solution, a place in the group home or the day center with its associated therapies, activities and routines. Good form now demands a sustained network of relationships in which good support can emerge and be refined and renewed, one person at a time. Even when generally effective patterns of practice emerge –as they have for R-Arc in employment, supporting people in their own homes, and collaboration with people and families who want tailor-made supports– each situation demands customization, and relationships need continual renewal and repair of inevitable breakdowns.

Many accounts of innovation presuppose entrepreneurs who claim the space to invent and venture capitalists who risk investment in the early, uncertain stages of a promising idea. But R-Arc functions in a federal and state human service system which has little space that is not already claimed and managed from outside R-Arc and almost no capacity to invest in new approaches. If the archetypal garage where skilled and passionate people like Bill Hewlett and Dave Packard cooked up the next great thing existed in this system, it would be regularly subject to unannounced inspections to assure no deviation from a growing tangle of rules and any investment available would demand guaranteed delivery of outcomes specified in detail in advance. The politics of Medicaid funding currently swirl around the prevention of fraud, the eradication of risk and the demand that care be managed to minimize cost. The system invests more and more in policing compliance with complex details intended to assure health and safety and scrupulously justify every expenditure. Continual scrutiny threatens to suck leadership energy into a whirlpool of error avoidance that consumes more and more of the attention necessary for innovation to flourish. Creating the blue space to which the title refers becomes more difficult as it becomes more necessary. It is possible to imagine a blank piece of paper in order to plan with people, but moving to action means discovering new ways to use available funds and human creativity, and that involves finding a way through a fine mesh of spreadsheet cells and dense thickets of fine print. The competing commitments generated by the system make for slow-motion transformation, much of which is paced by try-and-try-again to manage the bureaucracy. R-Arc's story shows both the limits imposed by mistaken efforts to mechanize care and manufacture quality by inspection and coercion and the achievements that become possible when people encourage each other to resist its pull without putting the organization at risk.

The third reason to study this book makes it unique. Leadership fit for today does not dictate the shape that assistance takes but creates and maintains an organization that continually gets better at holding the work of generating and re-generating individualized supports. A key function of this kind of leadership is sense-making: discovering frames and patterns for thinking that guide useful action and allow learning. As Hanns Meissner's engagement with the search for good organizational form grew, so did his interest in theories and practices produced in the growing field of organization development. His bias for action has made him an enthusiastic tester of the usefulness of a variety of theories and their associated practices. An important part of his story of R-Arc's journey is what its management has seen through the lens provided by these theories and what actions they have taken based on what shows up from those perspectives. So this book demonstrates multiple theories and practices in use as R-Arc develops rather than laying out a single view or technique to explain its progress. As well, the frameworks offered by Otto Scharmer's elaboration of Theory U have inspired Hanns to create and explore an account of the development of the field of support to people with developmental disabilities that frames much of his current thinking and organizes the book.

But a careful reading of this book will show much more than the exposition of useful theories or a case study of long term change. It is the story of a continuing search for organizational forms that channel compassion into the practical work of people day-by-day offering one another the resources to live a life that they have reason to value.

John O'Brien

R-Arc Founders
Ernie and Henrietta Messier and their children

Back Row (left to right) Colette, Lori, Mark, Marty, Greg

Front Row (left to right) Ernie, Cherie, Henrietta

1

The Search for Good Form

Consciousness is an experience. It goes deeper and deeper into the experience, behind the mental constructs and behind the veil of your emerging tendencies. You come to your own natural wisdom. So intuition or inspiration is really the experience of your own wisdom. It is like seeing a small patch of blue sky amidst the clouds –and you try to widen that patch through personal transformation.[2]

—*Matthieu Ricard*

Creating a new theory is not like destroying an old barn and erecting a skyscraper in its place. It is rather like climbing a mountain, gaining new and wider views, discovering unexpected connections between our starting point and its rich environment. But the point from which we started still exists and can be seen, although it appears smaller and forms a tiny part of our broad view gained by the mastery of our obstacles on our adventurous way up.[3]

—*Albert Einstein*

Over the past thirty years, my perception of people with developmental disabilities has deeply shifted. I am currently an executive of an agency grappling with how to assist people who have been historically excluded from our communities to experience ordinary, if not extraordinary, lives. My connection with The Arc of Rensselaer County (R-Arc) began in the era of deinstitutionalization. There is no shortage of descriptions of how the care for people with developmental disabilities in the mid-20th century had degenerated into neglect and abuse. Burton Blatt's 1966 photographic exposé, *Christmas in Purgatory,*[4] and Geraldo Rivera's award-winning reporting on Willowbrook State School in New York,[5] were hard hitting illustrations of life in institutions that brought this injustice to our nation's attention. The consummate failure of the institutional system to humanely meet the needs of its population forced society to rethink how best to support people with developmental disabilities. Out of the death throes of institutions emerged solutions that greatly improved people's living conditions, but left them separated from our communities as service system clients. Now the leading edge of the field is discovering the next generation of ways to support people as contributing members of their neighborhoods and communities.

For more than sixty years, R-Arc has been part of this story as one of a cohort of providers concerned with creating and operating a parent-governed agency that supports individuals with intellectual disabilities in community settings. From its beginning, R-Arc has both embraced contemporary forms of group services, and resisted their prescriptions and restrictions by finding new ways to individualize support. Initiated as an alternative to large, often geographically remote institutions, our agency offered education and activities in various locations within our county but separate from its mainstream life. We have always been open to emerging positive trends in our society: increasingly enlightened beliefs about individual differences (ethnic and otherwise), greater inclusion of marginalized people in society, advances in health and educational technologies, new perspectives about holistic practice, and a growing value on autonomy and self-determination. These trends influenced our perceptions of support roles and service design. With years of collaborative effort, R-Arc has created a culture capable of generating support arrangements that assist people with developmental disabilities to exist as three–dimensional human beings, experiencing the full spectrum of life's offerings. These new practices, created by transformational leadership, can only be born and grown in blue spaces, where ethical action can thrive.

The Purpose of this Book

This book is primarily for organizational leadership, change agents, and policy makers interested in transforming services, agencies, communities, and systems in ways that promote real lives and social inclusion for people with developmental disabilities. To this purpose, I hope to expand understanding of how our beliefs about persons with disabilities shape our roles and relationships, the nature and experience of our practice, the design of our organization, the framing of our system, and ultimately the type of outcomes we achieve with the individuals we care about and support. Within the pages of this book, I will share what R-Arc has learned so far on the journey of transforming our group-based legacy services –a term I use with great respect to describe services that emerged to implement deinstitutionalization. Group homes, sheltered workshops, day treatment and day habilitation centers are examples of legacy services. It is important to acknowledge the contribution that these services made to correct the grave injustices of the institutional era and their position as a bridge to individualized supports. The history of my agency reflects our evolution from helping relationships shaped by health care experts to transactional relationships reflecting the provider-consumer dynamic, and most recently to a partnership relationship based in a process of co-planning, co-designing and co-implementing individualized supports.

Our story is far from finished; our evolution is incomplete. Not everyone we have supported has attained a life of accomplishment and citizenship. However, our story is worth sharing because of our relentless pursuit of organizational learning. We are becoming more attuned about how we can identify and manage our competing commitments, develop ourselves as instruments of change, invest in practices that support innovation as well as stability, and expand our willingness to collaborate with individuals and families.

I am writing this book for the person or team that senses the enormity of the social transformational challenge and is skeptical of recipes in books that lay out a few action steps to realize cultural change. For those that aspire to create nurturing spaces in which new and more diverse social forms can evolve, this book provides a framework for reflective practice focused on innovations of individualized supports to unfold in a self or team guided learning journey. It is my intent that others will consider our experiences and reflective processes and find ways to integrate what they find useful into their own practice. I hope this book will be a catalyst for evolution into a community-centered support orientation for all people with developmental disabilities.

Seeking Good Form

I have spent my whole life seeking to develop good form, in all my relations with others and in organizing support for people with developmental disabilities. I use good form[6] to express a process similar to the way a loving couple successfully manages a crisis while remaining whole and fulfilled as they navigate difficult conversations. Good form is also seen in the way a sculptor releases a human shape from a block of stone to reveal something essential about the mystery of life, or in the way an architect designs a building to host collaborative engagement, or in the way a pitcher's curve-ball delivery is an expression of letting go. In this book, good form refers to healthy human relations and effective organizations, and also the actual structures and processes that promote these positive conditions. All good forms, whether at the individual, group, organizational or system level, are fluid. Those with a positive purpose continually search for forms of relationship and organization that support their mission and vision in a changing time and place. This search contends with equally powerful and present forces of devolution that produce bad forms of human relations and organization and cause dysfunction, suppression of human spirit, and the destruction of community.

Much like the rest of the world, we who are committed to better lives for people with developmental disabilities are at a crossroad where the choice is between responding to all the surrounding turmoil with hierarchical command and control interventions, or transforming ourselves and intentionally building community. In spite of the storm of destructive forces surrounding us, I have increased my understanding that all living things possess the capacity to discover good form, one that achieves its most creative expression in the historical moment. The search for good form is as much an aesthetic process as a utilitarian one. Take note of a beautiful picture, a scenic mountain-view, a conversation that creates meaning between two people or a bridge that allows passage across a river. What is created aligns holistically with our sense of purpose, beauty and well-being. Good form also is instrumental in getting the results we desire. Thus, when the traditional institutional forms no longer work for people with developmental disabilities, both utility and aesthetics demand the invention of new support models. With this awareness, I have attempted to join with others in creating blue spaces wherein good forms to support our citizens with developmental disabilities are born.

Creating Blue Space

Blue space is the eye of the storm where living things flourish despite being surrounded by destructive elements of the universe. I adapt blue space[7] from American philosopher Philip Hallie's statement likening the eye of the storm to capacities for love and ethics notwithstanding human cruelty, a motif in his work exploring resistance to institutional evil. Acknowledging the moral complexities of individuals and cultures, Hallie urged people to expand the blue: cultivate a realm for peace and morality through courage, passion, resourcefulness and innovation.

I use this term to describe the inner-state of a person and the organizational containers that produce a creative energy that, in turn, translates into positive, life giving action. Service provider agencies like R-Arc are surrounded by demanding and potentially destructive political and market forces. If we, as individuals and organizations, are to create solutions to stuck social problems such as the exclusion of people with developmental disabilities, we must discover how to prepare ourselves to resist the crush of these debilitating forces and make room for generative actions to emerge and grow strong.

My understanding of how generative change emerges has been heavily influenced by Otto Scharmer's Theory U.[8] This theory of how innovation is expressed in our world functions like a software operating system in the background of this book. Theory U explains that innovation occurs by shifting one's perception from downloaded or deeply ingrained thoughts, beliefs, and routines to active engagement through seeing and experiencing the variety of life expressions surrounding us.

Scharmer believes that we must ignite our creative energy to bring forth a future that wants to be born by tapping into the internal source of our inspiration and deepening our connection with others. The U shape illustrates the trajectory of a deep dive into new ideas, experiences, and relationships along with inward reflective practice that connects us to our truest purpose and meaning at the bottom of the U. Ultimately, this deep dive prepares us to sense and create new and innovative ways to participate in community life. This is a path that I and The Arc of Rensselaer County aspire to follow.

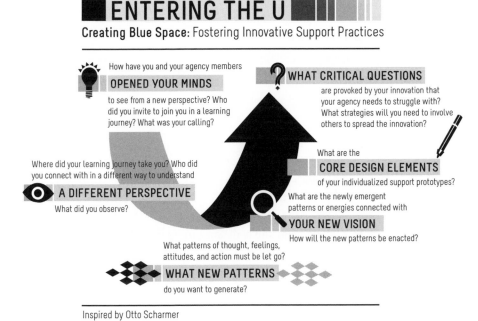

ENTERING THE U

Creating Blue Space: Fostering Innovative Support Practices

How have you and your agency members **OPENED YOUR MINDS** to see from a new perspective? Who did you invite to join you in a learning journey? What was your calling?

WHAT CRITICAL QUESTIONS are provoked by your innovation that your agency needs to struggle with? What strategies will you need to involve others to spread the innovation?

Where did your learning journey take you? Who did you connect with in a different way to understand **A DIFFERENT PERSPECTIVE** What did you observe?

What are the **CORE DESIGN ELEMENTS** of your individualized support prototypes? What are the newly emergent patterns or energies connected with **YOUR NEW VISION** How will the new patterns be enacted?

What patterns of thought, feelings, attitudes, and action must be let go? **WHAT NEW PATTERNS** do you want to generate?

Inspired by Otto Scharmer

Organization of the Book

This book explores three core themes: 1) The breakdown of the delegated approach to serving people with developmental disabilities and the search for good support forms through innovation in an evolving developmental disabilities field; 2) Moving from client-hood and consumerism to citizenship by undertaking a quest for communities of diversity and mutuality; 3) The design and delivery of individualized supports through the development of blue spaces that encourage generative action in self, relationships and organizations. These themes develop in four stages of evolving service and support models for people with intellectual and developmental disabilities: Institutional Care, Managed Care, Integrative Supports, and Community Supports. Each stage is defined by the particular ways it solves nine problems:

- How the culture of an agency creates core beliefs that guide support practices (Chapter 3)
- How the underlying design principle serves as the foundation for how services are organized and delivered (Chapter 4)
- How outcomes are defined (Chapter 5)
- How increased complexity and competing commitments are understood and managed. (Chapter 6)
- How leadership orientation develops (Chapter 7)
- How the roles and relationships between those who provide assistance and those who receive it change (Chapter 8)

- How assistance is delivered and experienced (Chapter 9)
- How organizational conditions facilitate the emergence and sustainability of individualized arrangements (Chapter 10)
- How innovation is generated (Chapter 11)

Key Points

- We are experiencing a breakdown of the delegated approach to serving people with developmental disabilities and the leading edge of the field is searching for good support forms through innovation in an evolving developmental disabilities system.
- There is a move from client hood and consumerism to citizenship as we and the people we support undertake a quest for communities of diversity and mutuality.
- The design and delivery of individualized supports is brought forth by the development of blue spaces that encourage generative action in self, relationships, and organizations.

Self, Peer or Team Guided Learning

If you are interested in transformational change at the local agency level, you can start by initiating a self and/or team guided learning process in concert with reading this book. As you respond to a calling for individualizing supports and social change, identify peers and allies to join you in a deep dive into "the U." A great way to start is to invite self-advocates, family members, agency leadership (including top administrators and board members), direct support professionals, and relevant governmental policy makers on a learning journey of individualized supports innovation. Tapping into the perspectives of all the key stakeholders is critical to create a shared understanding about what is holding your agency and the system back from implementing a form more conducive to individualized supports.

The learning journey can be of great value if it includes a real life project of individualizing supports for a person currently served in your agency legacy settings. It can be of equal value as a self or peer guided reflective journey if it moves you partway down the "U" in an effort to deepen your understanding of the dynamics of individualized supports (possibly increasing your readiness for transformative change in the future). To assist readers who choose to embark on either learning pathway, the chapter summaries contain practical and reflective exercises to consider alongside the nine problems previously outlined.

Starting the Self/Team Guided Learning Journey

Identify a study partner or members for a diverse learning team. Your study partners must all share a vision of real lives for people with disabilities, a passion for reflective practice and a calling to evolve supports. Try to include self-advocates, family members, agency leaders, direct support professionals, interested community members, and relevant policy makers in your learning team. This should be a voluntary activity.

1. Invite your partners to prospectively envision the "U" journey you are about to undertake. Get familiar with Theory U by reading the executive summary on the Presencing website: http://www.presencing.com/executivesummary. Read up to this page to understand the components of the learning journey (the nine problems offer a learning framework to consider supports transformation). Reflect on the questions listed in the "U" graphic on page 17. Share your response with a peer or your learning team.

2. In a self-reflective, peer or team process, perform exercises *1: Discovering the Resources in Our Community of Practice* (page 158) and *2: Deepening our Skills as Innovators of Individualized Supports* (page 159). Both exercises are located in the appendix.

3. Develop a learning agreement with yourself, a partner or with the team. You will first need to decide whether the learning will be pragmatic, i.e. an innovative supports project with a person your agency currently serves, or a reflective journey. Then, you can determine the scope of the learning journey: Is it a book group? Is it a project change team? Is it a circle of support designing an individualized support arrangement? In other words decide whether the learning will be practically based in terms of an innovative supports project with a person your agency currently serves or a reflective journey.

4. Record your reflections of the guided journey in a journal. See (page 189).

2

The Intentional Journey to Individualize Supports

Social inclusion for individuals with developmental disabilities has been difficult. Our service practices often miss the mark in connecting people to valued roles in their communities. With good intentions and often with great professional competence, R-Arc and other service providers have produced program experiences in segregated group settings rather than facilitating natural life experiences. Yet something is changing. As most of the younger generation is included in their schools, the demand for more typical life trajectory grows. Consider the difference between these recent accounts of service planning at R-Arc:

> *Sue has been invited to sit in on her individual service plan meeting for the first time since she began receiving day and residential services in 1980. In a prior life, Sue lived in a state institution until she was repatriated to her county of origin at the age of twenty-five. Experiencing the transition from a state school to a group home was a profound liberation from a contained existence, moving from a sterile environment into a comfortable home, much like many other young women in their mid-twenties, with a roommate and six others on a tree-lined street. Though this transition was a significant step in the right direction to a more inclusive, normalized life, Sue felt emotionally disoriented. Gone were the oppressive features of institutional life, now replaced with a small group setting with caring staff. A work center during the day provided her with a small pay-check and a sense of contribution and belonging. Over the years, staff structured a program and set of goals for her to work towards based on periodic assessment of her needs. Sue was being seen as a person, with goals, dreams and desires. When asked how satisfied she is with staff and the agency that supports her, Sue's response has always been positive.*

Despite the overwhelmingly positive changes, Sue's life still lacks the elements other people take for granted: real, unfettered freedom and authentic human connection. Instead of choosing her own path, Sue's day-to-day life is completely structured by others. She lives with people she would not live with if given a choice, and relies on the guidance of people, though caring, who are paid to befriend her. Intimate relationships have not had the chance to organically blossom the way she witnesses other's experience, or in the ways media and television portray friendships. Beyond a hello to familiar clerk or employee at the local stores, movie theaters and the work center, Sue is not connected to her surrounding community. Her intuition tells her that she is missing something significant as she listens to her staff discuss her "programming."

> *In contrast, Bill is graduating from the high school in which he has been mainstreamed with typical children throughout his schooling. He has been surrounded by a circle of support during his transition years who have encouraged age-typical activities in his community, leading to authentic experiences, some fulfilling and successful, others difficult and challenging. People in his circle of support assisted him in finding a stimulating work-study arrangement, in joining various school clubs and participating in sports, where Bill has developed relationships with peers based on shared interests. Moving into the next phase of life, with the help of his parents, Bill looked into a supported college experience, where he would live on campus among other's his age, engage in classes, and hold a part time job. Of course, Bill is especially interested in meeting young women and widening his experience of dating and the joys of romance. After persistently searching, Bill and his parents finally found a community agency willing to support Bill's vision of life as a college student. The agency is willing to negotiate how the support tasks are shared with his circle, which includes committed friends, service professionals, and his parents.*

Something is Shifting

Something is shifting in the conversation between people seeking services and those who are charged with their ongoing support. At individual planning meetings in our agency, we increasingly hear people express a desire to live a life. "Living a life" usually means: having health, a job, a family and friends, a place to call home, and a strong connection to community. People expressing their true desires have recalibrated our traditional ways of viewing persons with developmental disabilities, their place in our world, and how to arrange supports. But as well-meaning human service professionals we can get trapped within a client-provider dynamic. We often decode the desire for assistance to lead an ordinary life into a request for placement into a service. When we see Bill as a client in search of a programmatic intervention, our ability to act in partnership with Bill and his circle is severely compromised. If Bill does not shrink his vision to fit what is available, he, his circle, and provider staff will find themselves talking past each other, each confirming preconceptions of the other as unreasonable and unresponsive.

The call for individualizing supports is growing louder and more assertive from families, self-advocates and government policy-makers. Many mission-driven agencies find themselves criticized for serving people in choice-constrained, non-inclusive, group-based service environments that offer people little control and few opportunities to live a full life. A common pattern in human experience traces the way one's strengths can also become one's weaknesses. As expectations shift, the status organizations may have once enjoyed as liberators of people from institutional containment slowly fades away. Today, programs that served the interests of refugees from institutions now look more and more like mini-institutions, undesirable and unsustainable.[9]

As the new century unfolds, individualizing supports are seen as the antidote for the over-responsible, highly segmented, standardized, costly, and hierarchically administered developmental disabilities service system. This idea is now more than twenty years old, yet the practice of individualizing support has not been widely implemented by the organizations that grew in response to deinstitutionalization. This inertia exists even when the benefits of individualized supports are clear and we have the means to adopt the practice on a larger scale. In many places, terms such as person-centered and individualized serve more as public relations sound bites than descriptions of actual offers of support. The journey to individualizing supports remains a path seldom traveled despite the expectations of growing numbers of people and families and the expressed intentions of those who administer the developmental disabilities service system.

Why is a widely desired and reasonably well-understood approach so difficult to move into the mainstream of our services? Simple explanations fail, in part, because they do not recognize the transformative nature of the change required. Enabling people with developmental disabilities to live a life as contributing citizens demands deep change in every dimension of a system to which most providers have successfully adapted. It calls for different relationships, service offerings, forms of innovation, ways to deal with complexity, uses of authority, and leadership orientation. Those who don't appreciate the depth of change that is needed can fall under the spell of the illusion that they are making good progress on the journey to individualizing supports when they are only wandering in circles within an outmoded pattern.

The Arc of Rensselaer County Story as Mythic Journey

Woven throughout this book is the story of The Arc of Rensselaer County (R-Arc) describing one provider's journey through the shifts in service and support in New York State from the mid 20th century until today. R-Arc's development offers a reference point for exploring how an organization evolves the capacity to individualize supports. Our agency's story can be told as a mythic journey in pursuit of a more inclusive community heeding a personal and organizational call to a higher purpose and a leap into unknown territory where the maps developed from past experience lack utility. Our path is evident in the historical development of physical sites and services operated by R-Arc. In its time, each of these forms of service expressed the beliefs of R-Arc leaders about the best possible response to people with developmental disabilities and each has contributed to our ever-emerging culture. Reflection on this journey and the conceptual frameworks we have found helpful in shifting our perceptions may inform other organizations seeking to individualize supports.

Beginning the Journey

The Arc of Rensselaer County originated at a time when institutions were the primary service option for people labeled as "mentally deficient." In 1950, when the Capital District Chapter of the New York State Association of Retarded Children was founded, it was a radical act to keep children with disabilities at home as opposed to shipping them off to an institution. Around the world, family based organizations like R-Arc were built on the hopeful visions of parents who envisioned their children as capable and contributing members of an acceptant and inclusive community – living, loving, and working beside neighbors, friends, and families. The formation of the Capital District Chapter of the ARC provided an opportunity for parents to talk about and plan for ways to support their children who were excluded from typical places in the community such as schools and workplaces. At that time it was public policy to exclude children who were unable to "benefit" from public instruction. Early support strategies of the Capital District Chapter, and later the separate Rensselaer County chapter, fell short of the vision of full social inclusion as the training or activity centers R-Arc created were housed in the free space of church basements and vacant community buildings such as the Acadia Building in Frear Park and School 10 in Troy, New York. The training centers provided some educational instruction, but mostly crafts and recreation. These formative activity centers were not funded by government dollars, therefore parents and friends engaged in many fundraising activities such as bake sales to cover program expenses.

The Rensselaer County Association for Retarded Children separated from the Capital District Chapter in 1965. By 1969, the recently formed chapter had opened Pinewoods Center, a school that provided instruction for children with developmental disabilities of all ages, including some adults. The operation of Pinewoods Center reflected the belief of the parents that their children could, in fact, benefit from instruction. Coupled with this strategy were intensive advocacy efforts by the R-Arc board members aimed at school districts, the state legislature, and the United States Congress to require public funded education for all children regardless of disability level.

Later in 1969, R-Arc implemented an "integrated" social-recreational program for adults. Not so integrated, this program supported groups of people with DD in recreational offerings in the community. In 1971, this program was expanded to include a summer camp, which continues to operate at the Tamarac High School in Brunswick, New York, that now includes children both with and without disabilities. A few years later, in 1974, R-Arc opened one of the first community residences for adults with developmental disabilities in the State of New York. This residence included people who were repatriated from an institution to their county of origin. Although some public funding became available for segregated programs in the community from the Department of Mental Hygiene prior to 1974, it was the opening of this residence that marked the time when funding from a governmental source (local and state) began to support individuals with developmental disabilities in Rensselaer County.

Major Legislation Supporting Inclusion

A major breakthrough with respect to public education of school age children occurred in 1974 when new federal laws (Public Law 94-142) articulated the responsibility of local school districts for the education of all children regardless of handicapping conditions. Although not all ARC chapters in New York State stopped running segregated schools, our Board of Directors immediately turned over education for children with developmental disabilities to Rensselaer County school districts based on their strong beliefs about inclusive communities. Pinewoods Center continued for a few years as an activity hub for adults then turned exclusively into a center-based pre-school for young children with developmental disabilities and delays. In 1982, Pinewoods Center was expanded to include an early intervention service (R-Arc Home-Based Program) that offered supports to parents and young children at home and in typical day care. This service started when the child was born and still in a hospital neonatal unit and continued in the family home until the child was three years of age when pre-school or day care began.

In 1986, R-Arc expanded resources to families with children at home through its Family Supports Program. The philosophy of Family Supports was to assist families to provide for their child at home in healthy and holistic ways. Case managers helped to connect families to service resources, and special programs such as family reimbursement provided families with stipends for things they identified as necessary to support their child at home.

Pinewoods Center closed in 1998 due to a saturation of children services providers in the Capital District and a change in reimbursement methodology that reduced funding. However, prior to this, R-Arc was moving its supports into day care settings as part of a strategic agenda to integrate its services into community settings.

R-Arc's adult programs evolved from activity centers based on an educational model that followed a school calendar to a vocational training program similar to the 1950s' rehabilitation programs aimed at disabled veterans and people injured in industrial accidents. Starting in 1977, R-Arc went through a number of sites for its vocational training programs, finally settling in a building at 484 River Street and a cooperative crafts store on State Street in Troy. The early years were challenging due to a lack of knowledge about how to run a business and provide consistent work in a sheltered setting for people just relocated from institutions or kept at home away from the mainstream and unaccustomed to work. By early 1979 when I joined the agency as a personal adjustment training counselor, the work center established its identity as Riverside Enterprises, a subcontractor to businesses for assembly work, a wire-forming and bending operation, and a packager of powder products for the State of New York.

Developing New Program Models

Never static for long, we took two divergent pathways to day supports in 1981. One path led to the development of a group day treatment program (a clinical/educational day care model) for adults we assumed could not engage in work. The other was the recruitment of a coordinator of alternative vocational programming who was charged with developing vocational options outside of a sheltered setting. This resulted in job placement, supported employment, and some work enclaves in local businesses. We eventually became known for working with "more challenging" individuals in supported employment, people whom other agencies typically served in sheltered workshops and day treatment programs. The day treatment program (later renamed to reflect the shift to day habilitation funding in 2001) pushed the limits of the funded model by finding individual volunteer work for many of its participants on a weekly basis in local non-profits and paid work in businesses outside the center walls.

In 1992, Riverside Enterprises intentionally reduced its census by over 50% (158 to 70 participants) through a downsizing initiative that both expanded our supported employment program and birthed our Community Inclusion Project, one of the first individualized day habilitation programs without walls (i.e. not centered in a service building) in New York State. Over the years, many of our new referrals have come from a School-to-Community Transition program, which was developed through collaboration between R-Arc staff member Carol Blessing and Troy school district principal Linda Martin in 1995. Students graduating from schools were primarily directed to our supported employment and individual day habilitation services given Riverside Enterprises' policy on capping enrollments at the downsized level. We tried our hand at enclaves –segregated small work groups of people with DD– in various businesses throughout Troy and Albany. Shortly, we gave up this strategy because it failed to integrate its participants into a natural workplace. Our primary investment is now in supported employment and individualized volunteer opportunities. Over the years, some congregate care funds have been reinvested in individualized day supports for a few people. Recently, we have gathered and bundled unutilized day and residential resources to support a number of people in individualized 24/7 support arrangements. We have labeled this "seamless services."

Creating Community Residential Options

R-Arc continued to open group homes that typically supported six to eight individuals each year until 1988. The R-Arc Board of Directors purposefully avoided the intensively medical modeled ten to fourteen-person Intermediate Care Facility (ICF)* in favor of more home-like settings serving smaller numbers. Initially, many of our group homes had shared bedrooms, but this practice was stopped in the mid-1980s

---

*New York State opted into the Federal Medicaid option Intermediate Care Facilities for Individuals with Mental Retardation in 1974. ICFMR is an optional Medicaid benefit that enables states to provide comprehensive and individualized health care and rehabilitation services to promote functional status and independence.

when we methodically eliminated two-person bedrooms. This was an acknowledgment that adults needed their own personal space. In 1983, R-Arc made a commitment to individualized living arrangements and opened four supported apartments (a less than 24 hour-7 day a week support model.) This began R-Arc's journey to its position as the largest provider of this type of residential support in New York State, proportionally.

Intentional Act of Individualizing Supports

R-Arc's 1988 strategic plan directed its administrators to downsize its group settings. As previously mentioned, Riverside Enterprises' work center was downsized by fifty percent, after which referrals and investments were directed towards integrated employment and volunteer work. The day treatment program was capped at 105 people and efforts were made to support people in limited volunteer and employment opportunities in the community and some small resource reinvestments were made to support individualized arrangements. For residential services, this strategy resulted in capping new residential development at three-person homes, continuing to open supported apartments, and a slow process of downsizing and then closing group homes to reinvest resources to individualized residential alternatives.

The agenda to develop small and personalized living arrangements has dominated R-Arc's strategic orientation throughout the 1990s and into the 21st century. The closure of the 10-person apartment building located at Prout Avenue in Troy signaled R-Arc's determination to systematically phase-out group settings and offer individualized support arrangements. This particular residential redesign effort gained the attention of The New York State Office of Mental Retardation and Developmental Disabilities (OMRDD)*as a Search for Excellence project. Another highly innovative effort initiated in 1993, taking five years to implement, was the residential collaboration with the Hall family to support their two sons. A first of its kind in New York State, the Hall/R-Arc collaboration was unique in its structure. The Hall home was converted into a two-family residence with the parents living upstairs in a space converted into an apartment and the adult sons living in an apartment downstairs certified as an Individual Residential Alternative (IRA.) The long incubation period was due to the blending of owned personal property and a certified residence, which confounded the legal department of OMRDD. Once the legal and regulatory issues were resolved, this arrangement became a living example of co-designing services with families and individuals.

From 2003 to the present, R-Arc has pursued creative residential arrangements with shared living, live-in and live-next-to supports, and paid neighbors. All of these types of support promote the concept of self-direction, where the individual experiences greater degrees of autonomy and decision-making. R-Arc obtained additional state

---

*In 1978 The Department of Mental Hygiene was reorganized and The New York State Office of Developmental Disabilities (OMRDD) founded. The name was changed in 2010 to the Office for People with Developmental Disabilities (OPWDD).

funding (*Options for People Through Services – OPTS*) in 2006 to convert nearly half of its residential services to self-directed and co-designed supports. In 2009, R-Arc participated in OMRDD's self-determination initiative by assuming Support Broker, Fiscal Intermediary, and ongoing support roles for individuals self-directing their resources. As of 2013, we continue to work at closing group homes and reinvesting resources in individualized supports. Most new arrangements with people are individualized and self-directed. In our legacy programs, we continue to identify unused legacy resources to shave off here and there to develop an individualized arrangement one person at a time. Our journey in transforming our group services to individualized supports is documented in a Center for Human Policy case study report.[10] The table compares our day and housing supports opportunities of 1988 with our 2012 group to individualized array of supports.

Growth in Individualized Supports			
	1988	**2012**	**Change**
Group Housing			**–17**
5-8 people	79	39	–40
3-4 people	0	23	+23
Individualized Housing Support			**+98**
Supportive & Supervised Apartments (1-2 people)	15	97	+82
Self-Directed, Shared Living	0	16	+16
Group Day Services			**–86**
Work Center	169	68	–101
Day Habilitation/ Day Treatment	102	95	–7
Community Inclusion (≤4 people)	0	22	+22
Individualized Supports			**+108**
Supported Employment	0	60	+60
Individualized Day Supports	0	48	+48

Our Primary Lessons

These are the primary lessons we have learned so far along the path to individualizing supports as they have evolved within a nested environment of local, state, national and global contexts. Some of these lessons may be unique to organizations like R-Arc, while others more generally applicable. All have had a significant impact on how our practices at the individual, group, and organizational levels have taken shape.

- The effectiveness of a service or support form that meets the perceived needs of one generation will, after a time, decay and require another form that works for the next generation. To a significant degree the new generation's expectations arise from the previous generation's successes and frustrations with the ability of a service form to meet their needs. We see this in the social architecture of legacy services, as it is not the best form to produce citizenship-related outcomes (home, health, employment, affiliation) for individuals with disabilities.

- A broad theoretical framework reflecting a prevailing worldview complete with a valuing system and a belief structure (referred to by some as a social paradigm) organizes what we do about, for, and with people with disabilities. These beliefs, in turn, influence the shape of a service or support and what kind of personal, relational, organizational, and community outcomes are possible. The search for a better form involves becoming conscious of a prevailing world view reflected in current reality, the limitations this frame of reference places on our efforts, and the purposeful search for alternative ways to understand our world.

- We live in a world of opposing trends. There are forces advancing an evolution to a more enlightened state in which people are more consciously connected and more self-directed while at the same time other powerful forces are producing devolution into hierarchical control and standardization with a declining tolerance of freedom and difference. This sets up a dynamic of on-going competing commitments and double binds in an organization's environment.

- Given a world of competing commitments, organizations must actively balance innovation and stability. This means developing an ambidextrous capacity to manage everyday operational concerns shaped by legacy service forms while generating new approaches to the core work that allow the emergence of new support forms.

- At the heart of individualizing supports is an enlightened relationship with families and individuals, nurtured and brought forth by appreciative inquiry and deep listening as opposed to prescribed clinical technique or methodology.

- Inventing new ways to relate and partner with individuals and families in co-designed support arrangements increases the likelihood of achieving valued outcomes that are sustainable.

- There are different possibilities for individualized support depending on whether its context is within or outside the boundaries of legacy services. Understanding these differences is an important guide to transformation.

- A deeper appreciation of valued support outcomes is critical to understanding what is important to and for an individual, defining provider roles, and designing an individualized support arrangement.

- Evolving to an individualized supports model calls on an organization to operate consistently as a generator of social innovations at the individual, team and organizational level.

- The deep change that is required to re-orient an agency and a system from legacy services to individualized supports is immune to rational change methods. It calls for creative expression to bring forth a future where people with developmental disabilities can be contributing citizens.

- A key theme in transforming legacy services to person-centered, individualized supports is to create an organization that fosters learning, collaboration, community, and contribution.

- Leaders need to individually prepare for the transformational journey from legacy services to individualized supports by developing themselves as instruments of change and to purposefully work to close the gap between espoused beliefs and true practice.

These lessons arise from a continuing journey motivated by a vision of a positive future world that includes and values people with varying capabilities. The journey is complex because R-Arc is part of a human service system that straddles multiple support orientations and enforces administrative structures that are misaligned with the system's espoused goals of providing individualized supports. This is additionally complicated by some people and families who see the move away from legacy services as a threat to their quality of life. Our journey is hopeful because the open minds, open hearts, and open wills of individuals and families, R-Arc's staff, and the people who manage the system have already opened a path towards this shared vision.

Key Points

- There are shifts in the expectations of people with developmental disabilities and their families about their services and their life. These shifts have to do with the desire for increased choice, personal autonomy, inclusion, and valued roles as partners, workers, and friends.

- These shifts can be accompanied by changes in the physical form of services and helping roles as depicted in R-Arc evolution as a service provider.

- The DD service system is profoundly influenced by dominant socio-economic themes in local, state, national and global contexts.

Guided Self or Team Learning Journey

1. Develop a chart or draw a graphic map of your agency's residential and day services: how they appeared in 1988 and how they are configured today. Make a clear distinction, if possible, between services that are group-based and those that are individualized.

2. Reflect on the chart and the development of services over the past number of years: What is different? What is the same?

3. What lessons have you learned over the years in designing, developing and implementing services for people with developmental disabilities? How are these lessons similar or different than R-Arc's lessons?

4. Are there people who are asking for more individualized supports? If so, would this be an opportunity to develop an individualized support arrangement as part of your learning?

Edie, Doug, Gary and Brian Hall's story is told in Chapter 3

3

An Appreciative Culture:
The DNA of The Arc of Rensselaer County

A movement is a self-contained part of a musical composition or musical form. While individual or selected movements from a composition are sometimes performed separately, a performance of the complete work requires all the movements to be performed in succession.

An art movement is a tendency or style in art with a specific common philosophy or goal, followed by a group of artists during a restricted period of time (usually a few months, years or decades) or, at least, with the heyday of the movement defined within a number of years. Art movements were especially important in modern art, when each consecutive movement was considered as a new avant-garde.

Social movements are a type of group action. They are the large informal groupings of individuals or organizations to focus on specific political or social issues. In other words, they carry out, resist or undo a social change.

Our culture has a profound impact on R-Arc, as it is the DNA that dictates the form of our organization and influences each of our decisions and all of our behavior. Our culture expresses our framing of the world and reflects the internal condition of our collective psyche.

Edgar Schein defines culture as:

a pattern of shared basic assumptions that was learned by a group to solve its problems of external adaptation and internal integration, that has worked well enough to be considered valid and, therefore, to be taught to new members as the correct way to perceive, think, and feel in relation to these problems.[11]

---

* Movements as understood in the arts and social action have informed my understanding of how the process of culture development has unfolded at The Arc of Rensselaer County. These definitions are from Wikipedia.

Organizational culture can assume many shapes and forms as it emerges in different contexts such as the four care models found in the DD world. Although there are exceptions, each care model often shapes a culture that fits its purpose (or defines its purpose). We see the Institutional Model as bureaucratic in nature with authority found in command and control. Those that have experienced services in Managed Care walk away with a sense that rules and regulations win the day. In the Integrated Model, if the culture aligns with the sensibility of this support orientation, beliefs reflect a strong affiliation between key stakeholders and an appreciation of difference. The Arc of Rensselaer County fits the later cultural form. The core of our culture embraces what is positive in people and the agency. We appreciate the capacities of all people (regardless of ability or disability) and the community. We believe we can change the world through an assets-based approach. We have an appreciative culture.

R-Arc, like other Arcs, was created over 60 years ago as an association of parents and family members dedicated to their children and kin with intellectual and other developmental disabilities. Early in our history, parents who bypassed the institu-tional option for their children coalesced into support groups. Then, these support groups created social and educational alternatives to the mainstream that excluded their children using whatever resources they could find in their communities. By the late 1970's the association's form had morphed into a full-blown provider organiza-tion as the energies of a core group of parents met the move to deinstitutionalization. The settlement of legal action to close Willowbrook Developmental Center started a flow of government funding for State of New York's programs to repatriate institu-tionalized individuals and critical services for the children families had kept at home. Bingo: one hand washes the other as parent associations joined with the state govern-ment in developing our legacy services. We now are a $28 million agency with 400 employees serving over 800 individuals and families.

It is in the accumulated shared learning of these families, and then later on of paid employees, that we see our expressed culture. This culture, in all its glory and blem-ishes, has shaped us into an agency that is positioned to create the next generation of support arrangements.

Our Founding Members

Our agency's founding members were struggling to cope in a world that excluded their children while simultaneously generating new ways to support them at home and in the life of their communities. Their process later merged with the task of de-in-stitutionalizing large numbers of people from developmental centers. The prolifera-tion of residential and day programs of our legacy services became the answer to the question of "how to support individuals with developmental disabilities?" It was a valid answer for the time and task, though in retrospect we can see that it was a more humane extension of the highly delegated institutional model. As such, it created an inherent conflict for the founding parents of R-Arc as they implemented programs that birthed the emerging professionalism of our legacy services. It was the struggle to integrate our founding parents' locally rooted values and beliefs of "small is beautiful" and "individual contribution and citizenship" with the cosmopolitan professional values that pushed standardized responses and numerical growth.

Early Movements

At R-Arc, this conversational waltz between the local and personal and the standardized and professional plays on, but looking back I can see a number of early movements that informed our cultural DNA. Each distinct movement involves a critical event in which a key R-Arc member successfully solves a problem. From these cornerstone experiences, the member arrives at a significant realization about a truth. This truth becomes embedded in a core assumption about relationships, reality and truth, and critical activity related to the mission of the organization. In turn, the core assumption is translated into messages to all newcomers, individuals, family members and employees alike, as they are socialized into the agency. Each movement leads us through one stage in the evolution of DD services to the next, and now currently to the edge of social innovation, where individuals are citizens and R-Arc professionals are partners. I am using the concept of movements both metaphorically and realistically to describe the culture-building process connected to thought, behavior and conversation of R-Arc members. The use of the term "movement" has been applied in history to describe social change, in music to describe pieces of a whole composition thematically linked, and to arts and literature to distinguish between forms of expression in different periods and to identify the avant-garde (or the leading edge of practice.) These various applications of the term movement describe aspects of the formation of the R-Arc culture. For the purpose of exploring how our agency's culture informs our edge practices, I bisect history by starting with the seminal experiences of our founding members.

R-Arc's founding parents, as powerful figures in the formation of our agency, played a key function in creating our culture by imparting their assumptions about people with developmental disabilities, and the community's role and responsibilities in supporting them. Through their high principles and determined role modeling, they taught others how to face the core work by defining the mission, vision, role, and function of the agency. What they taught us has helped us to deal effectively with what was thrown at us in the course of a day. It stuck like glue to our minds and informed our practice for the following sixty years.

The Germination of Our Story

Our story begins in the 1940s, before our Arc chapter was formed. This was a time when parents who supported their children at home did so against the advice of their family doctor. Prevailing medical opinion guided parents to send their child with an "incurable condition" such as mental retardation to a state "school." Those who opted out of this pathway did so as a result of answering a calling. Henrietta Messier, our R-Arc's founding parent, answered her life's calling when she and her husband Ernie decided to keep Cherie, their daughter with Down Syndrome, at home. This decision launched Henrietta on a hero's journey from which the lessons she learned are now woven into the cultural patterns of R – Arc. The journey unfolds in movements, each of which adds a vivid pattern to R-Arc's organizational culture. This is an emblematic narrative, in many ways representative of all the family heroes of the 20th century, and therefore is a story of how neighborhoods and our larger society began a transformational process that ultimately concludes when people with disabilities are full members of our communities.*

The First Movement – Rejection of Prevailing Thought

The first movement reflects a disruption of the social norm, an act of rejection of prevailing thought and action. The Messier family enjoyed living in the small community of Green Island, a tightly knit enclave located across the Hudson River from Troy, New York. But even in this friendly neighborhood, their deeply felt beliefs about family and community did not prepare them for the gauntlet of discrimination and exclusion that Cherie and other people with disabilities faced in the long march to today's world. From the time the chief medical doctor at the area hospital told the Messiers "to put her in an institution and forget they ever had her," and throughout Cherie's early years, the family and Cherie experienced devaluing social experiences. Even routine community and family tasks, such as obtaining life insurance and responding to census takers became rituals of exclusion and humiliation. Yet Henrietta and Ernie kept Cherrie home, rejecting the expert advice of the day.

The Second Movement – Making Visible the Socially Invisible

The second movement involves making visible the socially invisible – seeing individuals with developmental disabilities as people. As the story goes, a worker from the Federal Census Bureau arrived at the Messier residence to carry out their function of counting people living in the locale. In the process of the census-taking interview, the worker told Henrietta that Cherie, a person with a disability who was not going to school, would not be counted in the census. Schools through the decades of the 40s, 50s, and 60s excluded children with intellectual disabilities. Henrietta responded by forcefully stating that Cherie would go to school if the doors were open to her, and she is a person who needed to be counted. Then Henrietta blocked the worker from the door, and said "you are not leaving here until you count my daughter." Cherie was included in the count that day.

The Third Movement – Early Forays into Systems Advocacy

The third movement reveals an early foray into systems advocacy. The movement starts when Henrietta and Ernie attempted to get all their children life insurance. The agent, sitting on a couch in their living room, stated it would be no problem, except

---

* Henrietta Messier's stories were collected over years of working side by side with her and through interviews during 2010 with Susan Streb and Dee Kronau.

for Cherie because of her "condition." He further explained that Cherie, "because she was retarded, might, through a lack of judgment, run out in front of a car or something." In response, Henrietta challenged the insurance agent: "You can't exclude a child because they have a disability." Determined and nonplussed by the rejection, Henrietta pursued the matter with the regional office of the national insurance company. She was successful in getting the denial turned around and a policy was written for her daughter Cherie. Henrietta's action set a precedent for other families seeking a life insurance policy for their child with a developmental disability. And so, this event ignited Henrietta's life long journey as an advocate not only for Cherie, but for all people with developmental disabilities.

The Fourth Movement – Expanding Community Capacity

A fourth movement completes a full cycle of the Messiers' contribution to the evolving DD field, and R-Arc's core cultural themes. It expresses Ernie's and Henrietta's gift of creating association and building community with their family, friends, and neighbors. The movement unfolds as, Cherie, being part of an accepting and inclusive family finds that she has opportunities to make friends in ways that many other children with disabilities did not. The Messiers, being who they were, extended the welcoming climate of their family by building the best playground on the block and inviting the neighborhood children to play in their backyard. Ernie, a master of the building trades, constructed the great sandbox and a double-decker tree house with a Tarzan rope. Cherie quickly became quite competent at using the rope to swing into the tree house. She did this using a process that involved wrapping the rope tightly around her leg while she maneuvered herself into the tree house. Attracted by the great playground, children from around the neighborhood flocked to the Messier backyard to have fun. Seeing Cherie swing into the tree house prompted children to ask her to teach them the special maneuver. The Messiers had created a vehicle to foster association and community right in their backyard, and Cherie played a valued role in the process. This foreshadowed their role in creating numerous associations and organizations to support people with developmental disabilities and their families.

Though the process of forming R-Arc culture did not end with these seminal events, I would like to pause and take note of what endures from these early movements in our organizational DNA. At the deepest level of our organization, truths that guide our actions at the strategic, tactical, and operational levels come in a direct line from these stories. They are a source and means to communicate our basic assumptions, the taken-for-granted truths that we interpret as reality in our day-to-day actions and our long range planning. Abstracted from the stories that carry them, these basic assumptions can be summarized like this.

Basic Belief: Challenge Authority

- Disrupt past patterns
- There is more than one truth
- Truth is discovered rather than revealed
- There are multiple ways to manifest power; not only from role or expertise
- There are different ways of knowing
- Those in positions of power and those labeled expert might actually be ignorant

Which plays out in R-Arc's history in these ways…

- Interrupt the automatic decision to institutionalize
- See individuals with DD as our neighbors
- Parent knowing is different from clinical knowing
- Parents become influential as advocates

Basic Belief: Social Justice for All

- Moral commitment to the rights of individuals with DD
- Create a society or organization based on principles of **equality** and **solidarity** that understands and values **human rights** and recognizes the dignity of every human being

Which plays out in R-Arc's history in these ways…

- Advocate for laws to include individuals with DD in schools
- Deinstitutionalization and the development of community programs
- Shape and advocate for laws and regulations insuring civil rights for individuals with DD
- Support individuals in their own homes and jobs

Basic Belief: Small is Beautiful

- People not systems matter
- Humanity flourishes in small communities
- Family and relationship is important

Which plays out in R-Arc's history in these ways…

- Keep R-Arc residences and facilities small
- Emphasize individual vs group solutions
- Roll-back group programs: downsize work centers and residences

Basic Belief: We Can Make Our World

- We construct our reality
- In partnership we can create a positive future
- With a mission and vision we can create anything
- We are autonomous

Which plays out in R-Arc's history in these ways…

- Face challenges with proactive engagement
- Embrace organizational learning and development
- Work to bring forth the leading edge of our practice

Ever-Morphing Culture

After 1974, when paid staff began to outnumber volunteers, assumptions emerged to inform our actions, define outcomes and ultimately influence the texture of our culture. This process, more resembling an improvised jazz session than a classically orchestrated piece of music, involved the interactions between our professionally staffed agency, R-Arc Board of Directors, and the Office of Mental Retardation and Developmental Disabilities (OMRDD), a growing state agency formed in 1978 from the New York State Department of Mental Hygiene. As the founding members turned over the daily operations to paid staff, they continued to impart these core beliefs to the developing organization by their ongoing presence as advocates in an expanding community-based system. Henrietta Messier and Ellie Pattison were very active, along with R-Arc professional staff, in local, state, and national forums focused on DD policy and program development. Both quite influential in all these forums, they remained primary drivers of R-Arc strategy as members of the Board of Directors. They closely worked with early R-Arc administrators Jim Flanigan, Karen Myers and Mark Pattison in rejecting the medical model (Intermediate Care Facility) as a residential option, instead working to open some of the first community residences for persons with developmental disabilities in New York State in the mid 1970s. Peeking out from underneath this decision were the core assumptions concerning challenging authority (clinical in this case), small is beautiful (a small group home instead of a large ICF), and social justice (a concern that the ICF would be overly restrictive for individuals). This decision is a vivid example of the perseverance and passion of Jim Flanigan, an early Arc employee who continued as the Executive Director and spent his career challenging the political powers-that-be whenever our core values were violated. When I came on board in early 1979, I became deeply socialized in these governing assumptions. I learned quickly that with this dedication and energy, we could create a new world full of possibilities for people with developmental disabilities.

Influenced by Context

R-Arc was not immune to the powerful influence of the newly formed and innovative Office of Mental Retardation and Developmental Disabilities. This state agency, like the Arcs, was born out of the advocacy efforts of family members and the public outrage of the abuses at New York State institutions. Unique in its mission and passion for correcting social injustice, OMRDD worked overtime in establishing a regulatory base, a financing structure and a programmatic model to fit the needs and interests of the developmentally disabled population. R-Arc, like most other DD agencies at the time, took the lead from our state agency. We embraced some of the approaches incubated in the field and further articulated in OMRDD cubicles. We opened group homes, operated a sheltered workshop, and enthusiastically embraced day treatment as a valid option for persons with multiple and severe disabilities. When OMRDD was approved to use federal Medicaid funds for its programs, we were swept up in this revenue-enhancing bonanza. How could we resist? Medicaid fueled the development of legacy services, provided funds to pay staff, and helped us survive many tight state budget years during tough fiscal times. With revenue, however, came the baggage of Medicaid: claustrophobic regulations, medical model expectations and an addictive dependency on a lucrative funding source. Our relationship to Medicaid was riddled with contradictions. Yet, working through these contradictions further evolved our agency's culture.[12]

Mediating the Internal and External Tensions

As OMRDD became a more powerful actor and simultaneously more dependent on Medicaid dollars, a conflict in basic assumptions began to grow. This conflict played out in our first Medicaid funded service – a clinically oriented day treatment program. At the time, the OMRDD specified model seemed a good fit for people with multiple and severe disabilities. However, opening of this clinically based group program flamed the fires of an R-Arc conflict that still burns today: founding member assumptions – personal knowledge is fundamental, small is beautiful, we enact our world, and challenge authority – are at odds with professional staff's externally referenced assumptions about the clinical potency of professional occupational, physical and speech therapies and psychological services delivered according to a professionally defined and prescriptive program. As this conflict played out, those holding the R-Arc core values card have claimed that the day treatment program was "day wasting," "cookie cutter," and placed clinicians in a dominant role. Others note that people at the day treatment center were better served than before and the critics espousing social inclusion values offered no practical alternative. The tensions between the "professionals" and the "natural supports advocates" have played out in various scenarios over the years. In its most dysfunctional moments, a unilateral power-over orientation ruled the day, with family or professional assuming a more dominant role over the other. When R-Arc engages this conflict from the most evolved relational state, families, individuals and providers become partners in producing resilient arrangements, as opposed to provider-consumer relationships that continue to struggle over the power and control of service decisions.

By the early 21st century, R-Arc's revenue mostly came from Medicaid funding. By converting from state funding to the federal/state Medicaid program, we were able to create a fiscally stable platform for our agency. This was during a time when other human services programs experienced a series of budget cuts throughout the 1980s into the 2000s. Buying into the highly regulated and prescriptive Medicaid program was our agency's valid answer to surviving in and adapting to an increasingly turbulent external environment. This was, of course, the norm to which almost all providers gravitated. With the Medicaid program came increased oversight and focus on appropriately prescribing, tracking, and documenting services. The high price of a negative Medicaid audit created need for increased controls in managing our agency's resources. Against a constricted backdrop, our agency's core values played out in a dance with innovation and stability. We became competent at attending to regulatory compliance, maximizing revenue, while pulling off innovative prototypes.

Cultural Messages Impacting Organization Strategy

I clearly remember a critical event in our history when our agency held its first board/staff strategic event. The time was the early 1980s and the setting was our pre-school facility, Pinewoods Center. Held during a vacation week in which the pre-school was closed, the retreat provided an opportunity for the Board and agency administrators to work on organizational issues. Here, a need surfaced to expand the building space at our day programs. As the sheltered workshop and the day treatment center were nearing capacity and with new referrals coming every day, we recommended that we either find a larger location or plan for a building addition. Speaking to the core R-Arc value "small is beautiful," Henrietta Messier and Ellie Pattison responded that "in no way were buildings going to get bigger." Their assertion was clear, and with building expansion out of the question, we needed to find other solutions to our space concerns. After the meeting, the administrators – Ed Martin, Jim Blessing and I – were dumbfounded, almost paralyzed by the Board declaration that blocked the favored provider strategy of the day – grow, expand, get bigger so we can deliver more of the same. None of our cooked solutions held water for our board of directors, so we needed to discover alternatives. From then on, almost in direct opposition to the general orientation of the day, we sought new service strategies for our legacy programs. Thus innovation emerged as a new core assumption about how to evolve our support practices and since was embedded in our cultural DNA: "we can make our own world."

Enlightened Management Adds to Our Cultural Pattern

Although heavily dependent on Medicaid funding and the detailed rules and specification of program types that comes with it, R-Arc held to its cultural values of "small is beautiful," "social justice," "challenge authority," and "we can make our world." We enacted our organizational world through a hybrid of practice, combining social action values with enlightened professionalism. With more resources, staff, and complexity came a need for increased management sophistication. In 1983, I reached out to the Director of the Antioch New England Graduate School's Organization and Management Department, Dr. Nancy Howes, to design and facilitate a team-building session for our managers across the agency. I also retained Dr. Howes as an executive coach. This was the critical junction at which we began investing in organization development activities. At the agency level we built human resource and financial management system capacity. We also engaged in strategic planning, large group intervention (e.g., Future Search, Open Space Technology), survey feedback processes, and total quality management. At the team level, we applied socio-technical design to enrich work processes and jobs, and tried our hand at role clarification activities, team building, leadership development, and conflict resolution. At the individual level, we encouraged self-development, learning journeys, and taking on increasingly more complex job assignments supported by the coaching and supervision of managers. My own learning journey led me to pursue a PhD in Organization

Development[13] with the Board of Director's blessing and support. In turn I applied my doctoral learning in my role as the Associate Executive Director. During the 1980s and 1990s numerous employees attended the Antioch program for a Masters Degree in Management. Antioch Graduate School was revered for a blend of the practical with the academic and strong social justice tradition. At one point, we had so many people going to the Bennington, Vermont Antioch Site that we were referred to as the Antioch West. Enlightened management became a core of our organizational culture.

R-Arc's enlightened management understands the symbiotic relationship between people and our organization. My vision is of a collaborative and positive workplace community for everyone employed at R-Arc. This is realized by engaging and empowering our employees as a way to engender their commitment to the agency's mission and to the people and families we serve. There is a direct line from the organization development activities of twenty years ago to our overwhelming attraction to learning organization theory, and more recently to Appreciative Inquiry, communities of practice, and Otto Scharmer's Theory U.[14] All of this informs our process to create blue space for the learning and discovery of new ways to support individuals to attain real lives in the community.

R-Arc Culture Embraces Innovation and Learning

Another major cultural pattern in our agency is our openness to new ideas and influence. This quality encouraged and imported exciting new perspectives from beyond our organizational boundaries to the core of our operations. We displayed an ongoing receptivity to people and ideas that informed and enhanced what we were attempting to do as support providers and as managers. We sought out and welcomed advice and direction about our primary tensions. For stability, we looked to management consultants, fiscal experts, and fostered positive working relationships with state officials. We were also guided by progressive management theories on creating innovative cultures through enlightened leadership. For innovation in our support practices, we were mentored either directly, or through published papers; by Beth Mount, John O'Brien, Jack Pearpoint, Michael Smull, Lou Brown, Michael Kendrick and others. We traveled to agencies and conferences to learn new ways of supporting people. R-Arc leaders personally applied the tools and techniques of person-centered planning. I clearly remember co-facilitating with Carol Blessing one of the first person-centered plans done by our agency for Philip in his family's home in Stephentown, New York. Philip has since gone on to live in his own apartment and has a life style of his own choosing.

Informed by the Insights of Innovators

We began to deconstruct our legacy world infused with Medicaid architecture. One person we have relied on for a strong dose of social role valorization (SRV – a theory developed by Wolf Wolfensberger based on the idea that certain groups of people are deemed socially of less value and offers ways to counteract this process)[15] is Chris Liuzzo. We had engaged Chris as a SRV consultant/trainer over the years, so I was well aware of his service philosophy and passion for innovation. When Mark Pattison left our agency, we recruited Chris to further our agenda in downsizing and closing our group homes and promoting innovative practices. It was a purposeful and provocative recruitment designed to underscore our value orientation, challenge the status quo and develop alternatives to our legacy services.

This led to numerous support prototypes, many involving planning, designing, and implementing individualized support arrangements with families and individuals. These efforts are effectively led by the creative mind of Sandy Van Eck, our Director of Innovation and Design. Only an agency with strong cultural underpinnings could support the productive management of the competing tensions (i.e. those produced by consecutively generating alternative support arrangements) within an overheated regulatory environment. Deep leadership commitment at the Board and staff level, along with relentless persistence and an ambidextrous capacity to attend to stability and innovation helped locate a functional space between good intentions and over-controlling regulations. It was in this space that we discovered pathways to close group homes and reinvest resources in individualized supports.

When we are at our best, we engage the complexities and paradoxes of this world by avoiding an either/or operating strategy. Just talk with Edie and Gary Hall, parents of Doug and Brian. Both sons were a handful to support as growing children and their clinical profiles predicted their placement in an ICF once they reached adulthood. Both had intense behavioral challenges, sleeping disorders and a variety of other issues the best of the medical field could not figure out. Edie and Gary did not like the therapy-fused and overly restrictive ICF option. They believed that Doug and Brian would disrupt the house for the others living there. The Halls turned to R-Arc to design a personalized arrangement for their family. After numerous planning sessions, the in-law apartment concept surfaced and a decision was made to move forward. The Hall's single family home would be renovated into a two-apartment dwelling. Edie and Gary would take the upstairs and the boys would be supported downstairs in a certified IRA. Given that state resources would be needed to renovate and operate the IRA, approval from OMRDD was necessary. At first, our state agency was baffled by the project proposal, a first of its kind in New York State. OMRDD needed to run it through its legal department because we would use state resources to renovate the Hall's personal home. A contract was eventually developed that met the state's legal requirements, green lighting the project. The point of concept to implementation spanned five years, but R-Arc and the Halls persisted in their advocacy, challenging authority and creating our own world with innovation. To this day, ongoing respectful conversations take place between R-Arc and the Halls concerning Doug and Brian's support arrangements. And the boys, now men, enjoy living in their own apartment and receive their day supports there as well.

This story brings me back to another core belief – the value of partnership with families and individuals. We have engaged with many more families to create a support arrangement that is unique in its touch and feel. This attention of working with families and individuals is a result of the instruction we have received from our founding mentors. We believe that our connections with families and individuals are at the heart and soul of our agency. The degree to which we stick to our mission can be measured by our relational well-being. The core assumption that defines family as critical to a support arrangement remains as true today as it has in the past. Standing with our families reflects a maturity of relationship and practice that positions R-Arc for social innovation and co-designed supports. We are finding good relational form in this process. This partnership orientation informs our collaborations with others in the community as well. The following chart shows the next generation of assumptions that have emerged from the ongoing process of R-Arc members successfully growing an agency's capacity for individualizing supports while dealing with external changes.

Emerging Assumptions				
Basic Beliefs	**Challenge Authority**	**Social Justice**	**Small Is Beautiful**	**We Can Create Our Own World**
Emerging Assumptions	Become ambidextrous: Balance innovation & stability Avoid either/or professionalism v natural support	Positive workplaces through enlightened management	Partnership & collaboration Relational wellbeing	Innovate: Find alternatives to legacy services

Key Points

- The culture of a provider agency emerges over years of interaction, learning, and action of a relatively stable group. The dominant founding members vision, values, and basic assumptions have an especially powerful influence on the organization's strategies.

- The lessons that an agency leadership group learns when successfully coping with the problems of operating an agency and providing effective services become part of its culture. What works will be taught to new members.

- The culture of an agency has visible characteristics, such as physical buildings, but the most enduring elements of its culture are the beliefs and assumptions of its members. These assumptions are often seen as the truth (about a host of things including beliefs about disability). They are often taken for granted and remain unchallenged guideposts for agency member behavior.

- The most powerful elements of culture emerge from interactions over time, are enduring, and taken for the truth. Therefore, changing the culture of an organization is difficult at best and often immune to rational goal-based methods of change management. Attempts to change the culture of an agency can have unpredictable outcomes or consequences.

Guided Self or Team Learning Journey

1. Who are your agency's early founders, how do their values, assumptions and actions inform your agency's culture (values, assumptions and behavioral expectations)?

2. Identify the basic assumptions that guide your agency's practices as they relate to service provision, relating to the DD service system, and your workplace. What do they mean? What do agency members believe?

3. Create a table of your agency's basic assumptions (similar to the table on page 44). How do the basic assumptions play out in the life of your agency?

4. Complete *Exercise 3: Supports Metaphor: From-To* (page 160). Evoking metaphors about your agency's current and future supports orientation is a way to gain access of deeply held beliefs and assumptions operating in agency's culture as well as a method to bring forth images of a more enlightened future.

Brian Aldrich (3rd person on the left) story opens Chapter 4.
Here he is hanging with his support person George Garin
(4th person on the left) their musician friends.

4

The Evolving Developmental Disabilities System

The essence of Theory U is the observation that form follows awareness.[16]

—*Otto Scharmer*

I wonder what the world will look like as I transcend to the next stage and look back on the world view that I have today. I am observing the blooming of myself...[17]

—*Robert Kegan*

Brian's service story starts when he was shuttled off to Rome Developmental Center soon after he was born in 1963. His Mom and his brother Wally visited Brian a few times during his stay in the institution. Brian never met his father and older brother. When a teenager, Brian moved to a smaller institution called OD Heck Developmental Center in Schenectady, New York. In the early 1980s, as a result of deinstitutionalization, Brian was transferred to the Hoffman family care home in rural Rensselaer County, New York.

In spite of being a boarder in someone else's home, Brian developed a loving relationship with Mrs. Hoffman. However, this placement was short-lived, and he was abruptly transferred to another family care home. Soon after, this next provider opted out of family care, and Brian was accepted into one of R-Arc's group homes, feeling discarded, disconnected, and rejected. Brian became difficult-to-serve, as he occasionally fled the group home, and expressed deep anger and depression. He was identified as "an elopement risk."

George, a direct support professional and house-manager, struck up a relationship with Brian. He remembers planning sessions where Brian expressed his dream about a house with a white picket fence. George eventually decoded this as Brian's desire to find his way back to the family care home. It was the close relationship with the provider in a warm, familial environment that Brian craved. With this insight and a personal connection to Brian, George worked with R-Arc to develop an individualized living arrangement.

Brian currently shares his life with George. The home is considered as much Brian's as George's, and his experience has now expanded to his connections with the community. He is an active player in an old time band and a recognized member of his church. Finally arriving at what he now considers his home, Brian's journey spanned four significantly different approaches to providing supports.[18]

The narratives of Brian and R-Arc's sit within a context of an evolving field of developmental disabilities services. The context includes the shared meanings and worldviews of our field and the larger society. Brian's current support provider George has evolved his perspective about disability and how to offer help in this world of changing contexts. R-Arc, as well, is as much linked to our own character and accomplishments as it is part of the evolving service system and societal culture in which we exist.

The Question: How Do We Support People with Developmental Disabilities?

Communities across our planet have struggled with how to think about, support, and include individuals who are disabled throughout the ages. How this question is answered is influenced by how we perceive a person with a disability. Our awareness of the capacities and gifts (or for that matter the deficiencies and shortcomings) of another person ultimately informs our response to that person. This perceptual process leads to a complex set of beliefs about a person's capacity to participate in community life and what constitutes support. These beliefs translate into visions, strategies, structures, and actions to respond to individuals who have traditionally fallen short of the social and performance expectations of the general population. This is the principle of the form of the support follows the condition of our awareness. Our awareness can either be narrowed by downloaded perceptions of people with disabilities or opened wide by listening deeply to another person and empathetically experiencing their world.

The last sixty years has seen an ongoing evolution of thought about people with disabilities, their participation in community life, and the role society plays in assisting them. During this period, our awareness of the gifts of people with disabilities has grown, and as a result, the forms of our services, relationships, and organizations have changed shape at least three times and a vision of a fourth form has come partially into view.[19] Those working on the edge of evolving practice assume that people with developmental disabilities have the capacity to live real lives as full citizens and so define their helping actions less as interventions aimed at individual deficiencies and more as providing needed accommodation and support.

The Perceptual Lens Shapes the Form of Services

At every level of organization from the individual to the larger society, people continuously attempt to cope and adapt to specific life circumstances within a prevailing worldview. A worldview operates as a taken-for-granted lens through which we interpret reality, truth, time, space, and other phenomena, including disability. It also is a schema that frames our values. If the interpretative lens works effectively, problems get solved, wealth is made, accomplishments lead to socially valued outcomes –life in general is good. If problems remain unsolved, unfinished business builds up, crisis reigns, leading a contingent of the population to look for a new approach. Should another approach work, a new lens forms our core assumptions, i.e., our taken-for-granted worldview.

The Structure of Evolving Practice

Models of care and support evolve when people open themselves to perceiving a more complex world. As our perceptions broaden and deepen, we see more nuance in our experience rather than rigid polarities. As people with disabilities are seen more like each one of us, segregated solutions come to make no sense. In turn, as we begin to see the world as inherently diverse and expressive in many ways, our community becomes inclusive. Furthermore, as we are able to see a more complex world, our models of support can grow and mature in tandem.

Emerging models of care and support transcend the limits of previous models by creating new ways to frame and solve problems. If successful, the new care/support model incorporates some of the effective elements of the previous evolutionary stage of care or support. For example, some of the things we learned about in-home assistance and job coaching in past stages can be useful when we support someone in person-centered ways. As new information, technique, and resources add to our ability to understand and support people, and in turn change how we perceive disability, we cross a threshold to a new worldview leading to an emerging form of caring for and supporting people with DD. New care and support models are elicited by the internal condition of change agents on the edge as well as provoked by environmental conditions.

Disruptive shifts in the environment –public outrage at abuse, budget crisis– influence the fit between current forms and environmental demands. So do alternative value orientations expressed by visionary leaders. As advocates like Henrietta Messier, leading thinkers such as Gunner Dybwad and Wolf Wolfensberger, and provider leaders like Hugh LaFave[20] attracted allies through their provocative positions, the firm ground on which the Institutional Model of care stood began to shake. As practitioners at the edge of the field discovered ways to support people with severe disabilities to do complex jobs, the assumptions underpinning sheltered workshops began to erode. These moments of awareness of the ineffectiveness of current perceptions and practices can be especially fruitful if we can open up blue space for innovation within them.

At any given moment, the service environment is fluid: many operate from the dominant perspective, some continue to operate from a worldview that most of the field has left behind, and some are purposefully seeking new forms that will allow better responses to emerging values and challenges. However, viewed from a distance, this dynamic process can be seen as a progression of stages. One worldview gives way to the next as institutional facilities are supplanted by community services, which, are then transformed into person-centered supports.

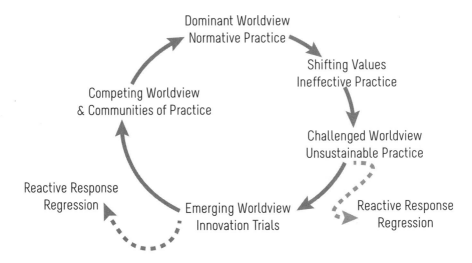

CYCLE OF EVOLVING PRACTICE

Individualization, as a practice, represents a new answer to the question of what form supports should take now that more people express a desire for a job, a home, and a life instead of treatment or a placement in a program. This is a result of a different perspective on disability and what it means to be a citizen. These more evolved beliefs about self-determination and individualized supports signal the need for a transformation of a current worldview and practices. Change is needed to move providers, individuals, their families, and our communities into a future support form that enables citizenship as a primary outcome.

Surfacing Deeply Embedded Assumptions about People

The primary leverage for system transformation lies not in policies, budgets, or organizational charts, but in the thinking and interacting of people in relationship with each other. To begin this transformational process, it is critical to increase awareness of our deeply held assumptions. In particular, assumptions, sometimes held unconsciously, about persons with developmental disabilities drive our actions in service design, and effect system financing and provider role orientation. If we see people with disabilities as tragic, vulnerable, and personally incapable individuals, our role will be to take care, protect, and assume full decision-making responsibility. Conversely, if we see them as inherently capable members of our communities, our role becomes one of partner in co-designing and implementing supports. These divergent world views of disability result in vastly different support delivery systems, so simply piling on new policies and practices without consciously examining and revising assumptions does not get to the level of transformative change that needs to occur if we are interested in citizenship for all people. Given this purpose, it makes sense to conceptualize and work with change as an emergent process where the seeds of a new evolutionary phase are planted, establish root, and grow into full bloom as the prior phase is decaying. This contrasts with trying to make abrupt breaks with a previous service form, a strategy that risks a strong counter-reaction and regression ("let's go back to the good old days").

The Evolving DD System

By the mid-1950's in the United States, a rising consciousness of human rights, growing professional interest, and expanding economies created conditions favorable to increasingly well-organized advocates for services to people with mental retardation, cerebral palsy, and epilepsy (formally assigned types and labels for development disability).[21] State and local government investment grew to supplement charitable efforts to provide local services offering schooling to children excluded from public education and occupation to adults. Federal funds initially supported research, professional training, and planning, but in 1971 the United States Congress authorized ICFs-MR (Intermediate Care Facilities Mental Retardation) as an optional service under Medicaid and changed the game with a massive influx of new funding. This funding, along with its regulations and practices, shaped the first stage of modern services to people with developmental disabilities: Institutional Care.

The table below, Evolving System for Persons with Developmental Disabilities, distinguishes four different approaches to organizing and delivering services and supports. It presents each approach as a developmental stage in the creation of better supports (Institutional Care, Managed Care, Integrative Supports and Community Supports). Each stage represents a different way to administer and provide services informed by an organizing principle expressing a particular worldview in the primary dimensions. When all the primary dimensions align within a service model, a dominant form is strongly expressed and coherent. Other times, the dimensions are misaligned revealing an emergent or decaying support form. The dimensions are:

- Individual-professional-relationship: how power is exercised and contact is established
- Service-individual interface: where and how the service is delivered and experienced
- Innovation mechanism: where and how something new is created
- Dominant form of complexity: how our world is experienced and where meaning is made
- Coordination: where authority is located and normative states emerge
- Infrastructure: what is the source for legitimizing and directing organizational activities
- Primary and emergent outcomes: what kind of results may be achieved
- Leadership orientation: how leadership thinks and act

	Institutional Care	Managed Care	Integrative Supports	Community Supports
Organizing Principle	System-Centered	Outcome-Centered Through Care Coordination	Person-Centered	Citizen-Centered
Individual– Professional Relationship	Expert-Patient (professional direction power over)	Provider-Consumer (professional responding power over)	Facilitator/Broker –Self-Directed Individual (individual co-designing with others, power with)	Resource-Autonomous Citizen (community supporting with professional auxiliary, power collective)
Service-Individual Interface	• Functionally Specified Services & Program Models • Model Driven (pull)	• Habilitation Pathways (core processes) • Coordinating Care Services • Service-Driven (push)	• Individualized, Wrap-Around Supports • Person-Driven (negotiated)	• Self or Co-Directed • Home & Community Located Supports & Resources • Community-Driven (allocation)
Innovation Mechanism	• Administrative & Functional Effectiveness & efficiencies (internal to the system) • Make Standard Products	• Outcome-Driven, Cross-Functional & Inter-Organizational • Deliver customized Services in Cost Efficient Ways	• Person-Centered, Inter-Organizational • Co-Created Personalized Experiences	• Citizen-Centered Community Based • Social Innovation • Support Individual Citizen Autonomy

	Institutional Care	Managed Care	Integrative Supports	Community Supports
Dominant Type of Complexity	Many Programmatic & Regulatory Details to Manage	Multi-Discipline Integration of Clinical, Financial, & functional Knowledge	Social Interaction Among Key Stakeholders from Different Cultures, Worldviews & Interests	Unclear & Unpredictable Futures with Understanding & Solutions Emerging from Action-Reflection Cycles
Coordination Mechanism	• Bureaucratic Culture • Hierarchy, Command & Control, Project Management	• Rules-Based Culture • Managed Care Entities & Care Coordination	• Affiliation Based Culture • Network, Facilitated Dialog & Mutual Adaptation (person-centered planning & future search conference)	• Collaborative Culture • Seeing from the Whole Through a Process of Collective Sense-Making & Innovation Cycles
Infrastructure	• Government-Driven • Social Legislation (laws, regulations, budgets)	• Corporately Driven • Rules & Norms to Make the Market Work	• Appreciative Inquiry Driven • Infrastructure for Learning & Innovation	• Collective Intelligence Driven • Infrastructures for Seeing in the Context of the Whole.
Primary & Emergent Outcomes for Individuals	• Placement • Personal Care, Face-to-Face Service • Activity & Housing	• Appropriate Service Levels • Reduced Cost for Services • Customer Satisfaction	Individualized Supports Leading to Jobs, Home & Relationships	• Citizenship • Life of Distinction (assumption of valued roles)
Leadership Orientation	Authoritarian/ Bureaucratic	Technician/ Problem Solver	Change Master	Generative Leader

Each evolutionary stage offers a distinct answer to the question: What is the best support form for people with developmental disabilities?

Institutional Care

The first phase, and still the dominant operating model in the field, is Institutional Care. Institutional care is a system-centered, fully delegated approach to serving a target population based on their deficiencies. Although all care and support models are potentially system-wide, Institutional Care is designed primarily around the system and a monolithic view of people. Institutional Care is not a matter of location or size. It defines many services provided in local settings –group living arrangements and day services– as well as larger facilities that are based on the expert-patient relationship and hierarchically managed and coordinated. Services are predefined and standardized, usually in program containers where the accuracy of placement decisions determines the fit between a person and the service they receive. The services are structured by detailed regulations based on a risk-aversion sensibility. It is driven by a view of persons with developmental disabilities as infantile, assuming their vulnerability to abuse and neglect. The outcomes that are valued at this stage are: placement in a safe setting, personal care, and programmed activities. An unspoken objective is to keep the community safe and unburdened by people with disabilities. The relevant governmental entities and service providers are charged with the full responsibility to care for all the eligible needs of this population in the least disruptive way to the community. Those in paid roles become expert at diagnosing needs, designing programs, and providing care for passive recipients.

The Institutional Care Model evokes an image of a machine. The machine image captures the sensibility of the bureaucratic organization that carries out the functions of Institutional Care; its purpose is to achieve quantitatively defined and managed objectives. Utilizing rationality and uniformity to trump individual differences and personal preferences, the machine creates rows of products without a glitch or fault. Institutional Care aspires to define practices scientifically, drive performance with data, and achieve cost efficiency, and its' organizational functions are arranged in pyramids. Tasks are divided into specialty areas coordinated through a management structure. To create this flawless product, work is carried out within the rhythm of plan, organize, and control cycles. Like any machine, this form fits well with clarity of purpose, routine tasks, and predictable and standardized outcomes that sit in finite and stable environments. It does not account for human beings whose "flaws" are markers of their character, individuality and personality.

In some ways, the machine method works when there are many details to coordinate in an institutional service. However, complexity is wrung out by standardizing processes and procedures. It is a simplified bureaucracy that operates with the assumption that the expertise already exists with the capacity to diagnose and solve any problem at hand. As gears of a bureaucracy grind on, its workplaces can devolve into dehumanizing, disconnected, mindless systems with the inability to adapt in rapidly changing environments. Referred to by Margaret Wheatley as "morbidly obese,"[22] bureaucratic systems can grow too large, inefficient, and unresponsive to the changing needs of people they serve. As years go by the technology of the machine becomes outdated and requires an overhaul. When the main change strategy focuses on restructuring units, departments and the organization, an under-investment in developing people and teams often occurs. Restructuring the organization is implemented to the exclusion of developing appropriate mind-sets, culture, and people skills. Ultimately, a system managed like a machine fits a stable environment that rewards the production of predictable outcomes but is inappropriate for innovation and building personal and community capacity.

Managed Care: Innovations in Coordinating Care

The second evolutionary phase, the Managed Care Model, grew as many organizations began to provide a wider array of local services to more people (R-Arc is one of about 700 providers in New York State.) This move was fueled by changes to Federal regulations that allowed states to apply for waivers to shift money from Medicaid-funded institutions to more local services. Managed care is driven by a cost-efficiency agenda which shifts the evaluative eye from service provision to specific programmatic outcomes, reduced use of inappropriate and costly services, and customer satisfaction. In other words, it is justified as a more economical way to teach skills to people with disabilities that will remedy their deficiencies and treat their impairments.

The Managed Care Model has put more and more emphasis on cost-efficiency. As rapidly growing numbers of elders and people with other disabilities as well as people with developmental disabilities need long-term services, it is the growing cost of the care system that claims the attention of public policy makers. This has led to the importation of cost-control practices from the medical field such as care coordination, disease management, contractual agreements, risk-based payment structures, managed care administrative entities, and a mentality hell-bent on reducing the overall costs of care across a large population.

As a move is made towards managed care, the services delivered in the Institutional Model undergo the equivalent of a home make over. Managed Care's primary impact on DD services is the decentralization of services from institutions to local providers serving consumers rather than caring for patients, and the re-engineering of policies, practices, service delivery structures and financial arrangements of systems. Within this phase, provider roles are guided by business models that emphasize consumerism. This continues the delegation of planning, design, and implementation of services as consumer demands and provider responds. Imagine, instead of being given the option to choose from three house models to purchase, none of which feel quite right, you are afforded the opportunity to work closely with the architect to customize your living space from within a selected model. There is choice around where the children's bedrooms will be, and if the porch faces North or West, and which is the best couch for lounging while watching television. Rescuing you from draining your life savings in the process, the architect works closely with your vision, finding viable solutions to keep the dream within your budget. The final product is a home that feels closer to your ideal space, with some compromises in design for the sake of your pocket book.

Similarly, attempts are made to customize services for people with developmental disabilities by moving away from pre-determined programs to an array of service options that are not tightly coupled. The potential for optional features theoretically offers increased choice while allowing for diversions from high cost services. Complexity increases under managed care as multiple providers of direct care, clinical, and medical, must integrate the many ways of knowing a person into a care plan. The result is in the establishment of coordinating structures such as care management entities to ensure duplication is avoided and care is complimentary. Here we move away, in theory, from programs to service outcomes. Instead of being accepted into a "residential" or "vocational" program, a habilitation or care coordination plan is conceptually purposed to get an individual housing or a job. Although re-orientation from process to outcomes is espoused within the Managed Care Model, the view on the ground suggests there is much work to be done to more clearly define and measure personal outcomes, especially when applied to an individual's life (exempting the mostly measurement-friendly health-related outcomes).

Unfortunately, as new solutions go, the Institutional Model lingers in how decisions are made and the type of service or support a person receives in the Managed Care Model. It is so close to the Institutional Model, perhaps because it is not fully realized as an evolutionary stage. Experience shows us that habilitation services often morph back into programmatic containers.

Decoupling From Care and Wrapping Support Around Individuals

The emerging stages labeled Integrative and Community Supports arrive at completely reordered arrangements based on power shared relationships, enabled by democratic or collaborative coordination and management styles. Care becomes support in the Integrated Model and individuals are viewed as having capacity and competency for community living. The infrastructure has deep roots in civil rights, democracy, and social constructivism. In this vision, spaces are available for providers, community members, government representatives and local businesses to develop common understandings, learn, innovate and implement new service orientations (including ongoing personal assistance and specialist professional service co-financed by specialized and generic payments).

Networks and collaboratives are organizational forms that engage key stakeholders in co-designing and co-implementing supports. Bringing together a diversity of creative thinkers and specialized talents can spark new ideas for how to foster workforce flexibility and adaptability, balance short and long term objectives, and enlist citizens with disabilities and their families in decision making.

Providers assume primary roles like facilitator, broker, or resource-linker; support provision becomes a secondary role function. Families and individuals direct their own support arrangements in partnership with the provider, taking ownership of the journey towards becoming a valued member of their chosen community.

The Integrated and Community Support Models, best known as person-centered supports, are perhaps the most conceptually difficult for current DD providers to wrap their heads around. This is because they are the furthest evolved from the current forms of services, creating the greatest tension with the administrative requirements that still govern the funding and licensing of providers. I think of a jazz combo improvising in full tilt in the Integrated Support Models as "players" must employ deep listening practices to hear the notes of their counterparts, and exhibit flexibility to move fluidly with the unpredictable path of the music. Service design is an ongoing strength based process to understand the capacities of a person and their changing interests as they grow. The Integrated Support Model enlists a committed circle of friends and service allies to design and implement a unique set of supports that enable the person to achieve their desired outcomes. The band works together, with the presence of the audience, to arrive at an enjoyable and exciting listening experience. Much like each instrument in the group forging its own voice within the larger whole, each support in its pure form is self-determined and –directed, and reconstructed as circumstances change. Different players can lead or follow at a given moment as participants in a playful musical conversation that gives freedom beyond each verse's structure. As integrated supports absorb the perspectives of diverse stakeholders, complexity is experienced as managing and integrating political differences. Somehow, out of the jumble of voices and instruments, a wonderful, challenging song is composed, thrilling in the sense that this exact piece will never be replicated or played again.

Where the Integrated Supports Model maintains a primary role for service providers, moving from system-centered to person-centered support arrangements, the Community Supports Model assumes that the individual is an autonomous citizen naturally accepted as part of a community. This approach omits the task of strategizing ways to connect people with disabilities to community because it values individual differences as critical components of a community's vitality, integrated and woven into the fabric of everyday life. A person then accesses supports when needed to sustain an interdependent life under their own roof. This is now a reality for the few that purchase personal assistance with government funds for helping in maintaining an independent life, such as individuals who have partnered with a progressive provider to create live next-to or live-in supports, as with paid neighbors (Mount and Van Eck, 2010). Overall, the Community Supports Model is more a vision for the future than a currently functioning developmental stage.

As the future cannot be reliably predicted, the Community Supports model replaces rational decision making processes with social innovation methods such as Theory U. Picture this model as an ecosystem: a vibrant balance of nutrients connected in their diversity. As new life forms come to fruition, the ecosystem evolves to accommodate them. In this sense, the responsibility to build an inclusive community is not centrally located in the provider or participant; it is instead symbiosis involving all stakeholders. When this is achieved, people with and without disabilities may co-exist as citizens with distinctive lives.[23] A life of distinction for individuals with intellectual disabilities involves their valued participation in employment, family, leisure, learning, and spiritual environments. This may resemble Nirvana; however, only from a distance. Complexity in this model is found when the authentic highs and lows of the human condition are examined and coupled with the future's ambiguity. Still present are the conditions of humanity including abuse, pain, loss, and suffering as well as the joys and pleasure of intimacy, contribution, and spiritual connection with others and the universe. The rich mixture of challenges and joys experienced give meaning to the trajectory of life as we engage in work and interact with family and friends.

For those who seek citizenship for individuals within an integrated community, the core question is how to disengage from a dance of competing commitments to choreograph a new evolutionary stage. This is the task for transformational leaders in all sectors of our society: in the household, in civic and governmental sectors, and in business and non-profit sectors. Social innovation calls for personal journeys of self-awareness, re-aligning relationships away from hierarchy to partnership, and transforming our communities to embrace difference. There are many sectors wherein certain types of innovation occurs; however, the most enlightened practice is birthed in blue spaces, created by people who collaborate beyond their niche, unbound and inspired by what distinguishes them. When we learn to move from our disability-defined spaces and roles into shared action on a common community agenda, individualized supports can join the mainstream.

What We Are Attempting is Big

Early in R-Arc's progress toward individualized services, we sensed that what we were attempting was big, and this was without having the perspective to view the evolutionary trajectory of DD services. Retrospectively, each DD support model describes a widely held standard and system of beliefs about "what to do with, and how to relate to, people with developmental disabilities." With the full spectrum the four support models' respective dynamics visible, we clearly see that we are in pursuit of a paradigm shift.[24]

Each support model is a best attempt at finding a good support form within particular beliefs and assumptions. The movement from one support paradigm to another is, by definition, disruptive to the status quo on many levels. If an organization like R-Arc, with many people and families who rely on services designed under previous assumptions, were to attempt to leap into a new developmental stage, there is great risk of invoking a destructive process that could wreak havoc in those people's lives. Destructive (or disruptive) innovation may be great for products, but not for people (unless an abusive situations requires a service to be to be immediately changed).

Evolutionary phases are not incremental linear steps; accordingly we must appreciate the vantage point cultivated in each stage as it informs the next, and bear in mind that fast-forwarding to the future is careless and will likely evoke more harm than good. This process is aided by an increase in awareness and engaged contact with our self and others, and a series of tests and experiments to find the right pathway. The act of inviting key stakeholders to learn about new ways to socially innovate opens doors for appreciative inquiry. In these conversations, we can see clearly the mismatches between our structures, relationships, processes and the types of outcomes we are becoming interested in creating.

Consider Loree's story as a living example of Integrated Supports, with perhaps a hint of the emerging edge of Community Supports.

> *Growing up in the rural part of the county, Lorree lived with her parents until she was thirty, and has always been an active member of the community. With a supportive family, Loree had many typical life experiences, including working for ten years in a day care center and a purpose-filled hobby of crafting with her mother. Though close to family, Loree's sense of independence led her to declaring her interest to move into her own apartment in Troy, New York. Given some personal capacity issues related to her intellectual disability, coupled with an anxiety disorder, her parents contacted R-Arc to explore support possibilities. Through partnerships and creative planning, R-Arc found an apartment complex where several other individuals were supported with "paid neighbors" arrangements. Loree and her parents achieved a win/win outcome, as Loree received the independence she desired, with access to supports during evening and weekend hours, as needed. Loree has been thriving in her apartment for over ten years.*
> *R-Arc's Community Inclusion Project, a without walls supports provider under the direction of Julia Kelly, connected Loree to various jobs (including self-employment as a potter) and educational opportunities (a computer class at a local college) in the community. Recently, because of her stated interest in gardening, Loree enrolled in a state sponsored intern program with a floral business. Everyone involved views Loree's process as a lifelong journey, with all of the ups and downs, textures and authentic emotions we each experience. Bottom line, Loree is living her own life in the community, the way she wants it.*[25]

Key Points

- The last sixty years have seen an ongoing evolution of thought about people with developmental disabilities. This evolution of thought occurs in stages and is practically expressed in DD care and support models that attempt to answer the question: What is the best support form for people with developmental disabilities?

- The evolutionary stages become apparent when the assumptions about the capacities, limitations, and degree of inclusion of people with developmental disabilities influence a shift to another care or support form.

- There are four distinct DD service models: Institutional Care, Managed Care, Integrated Supports, and Community Supports. The primary dimensions (i.e., individual/professional relationship, service/individual-interface, innovation mechanism, dominate type of complexity, coordination mechanism, infrastructure, primary/emergent outcomes, and leadership orientation) are differently expressed and uniquely aligned with each service model. Each care or support model is designed to get certain outcomes, and by definition cannot get others (the concept of misalignment).

- Understanding the care or support model that an agency and DD system operates within is prerequisite to initiating a change process.

- The movement from Institutional Care to Integrated Supports entails a big shift of thinking, relating, and acting for all key stakeholders. Creating blue space for supportive practice communities to prototype social innovation is a way to minimize highly disruptive and destructive change for people in current support arrangements.

Self/Team Guided Learning Journey

1. Review *The Evolving System for People with DD* (page 52) to gain an understanding of each primary dimension. Discuss how each dimension is defined and what form the dimension assumes within each care or support model with your partner or your team. Aim to achieve consensus.

2. Identify which evolutionary form of DD service model is dominant in your agency? On a flip chart, replicate the Evolving DD Systems table. In your learning group, identify the forms your agency assumes in each primary dimensions, using dots as an identifying marker. Are the dots that are most frequently placed align under one model or are they distributed among multiple care or support models? Reflect on the meaning of the dot arrangement on the chart for your agency, the people you support, your roles, your leadership style, and the scope of the transformation journey ahead for your agency. Do you see examples of different evolutionary forms in your agency? What are they? And how do they impact upon people's lives and the kind of support they receive?

3. Perform *Exercise 4: Core Assumptions Guiding Our Practice* (page 165) Identify for each question the actual functioning belief or practice you have (A), your agency has (B) and the desired belief or practice for individualized supports (C). Reflect upon your answers and what they mean in terms of your change journey.

Richard David (on the right) is the subject of a letter in Chapter 5.
He is standing with his former paid neighbor Larry Broderick
in front of Beth Mount's Key to Life Quilt.

5

Outcomes That Are Valuable to People

The privilege of a lifetime is being who you are.[26]

—*Joseph Campbell*

It isn't outcomes that matter. It's our relationships that give meaning to our struggles.[27]

—*Meg Wheatley*

Data and measurements are not half as persuasive as anecdotes… (which are) like biblical parables… through which faith is restored. The persistent questions about data and evidence are most often a form of disagreement, or despair or show a lack of faith. There is little discussion of faith in organizations, but it is only with faith that significant changes can begin.[28]

—*Peter Block*

Outcomes become valuable when they assume good form in our relationships at home, at work, and in our civic life. Discovering good form is as much an aesthetic quality as a successful accomplishment. Good outcomes express our most beautiful, creative self as well as achieving results that we value. Therefore, the most important outcomes are nurtured in blue spaces and defined by asking critical questions about our deep purposes as individuals, partners, groups, and organizations.

Perhaps unintentionally, the outcomes sought by services functioning in the Institutional or Managed Care Models tend prioritize system concerns as opposed to human quality. They are often defined and standardized in systems terminology, focused on populations rather than individuals, and expressed in terms of placement, treatment, disease management, support encounters, and cost efficiencies. In these models, inputs (e.g., encounters) are often masked as outcomes and the correlated accountability is delegated to the providers. Systems now are increasingly calling for typical life outcomes such as work, a home of one's own, and a healthy life of community engagement. Unfortunately, delivery is stagnated by contradiction: as structure, practices, and power remain stuck in Institutional Care or Managed Care, and they fail to develop what it takes to actualize authentic person-centered outcomes.

In Search of Valued Outcomes

As services and supports evolve from caring for people in institutional settings to supporting an individual in a rich life, outcomes look very different. Raise your hand if you can remember the language everyone once used to describe system outcomes. After you have muscled past the gag response, you may be able to spit out terms such as "slots" and "beds." Outcomes from this mindset primarily focus on providing care and face-to-face services. This systems-oriented language continues to describe services, which is fitting as our interests continue to ultimately emphasize a shift to efficient management of our resources with managed care.

We know we have accomplished something if the people we support have a career, and are enjoying close friends and partners, sharing their time with others in ordinary places, choosing how they live and with whom, and contributing to making their community a better place. Early in my tenure with R-Arc, valued outcomes such as these were blurred by the thinking and practice habits of the Managed Care Model. We were certainly great at espousing commitment to valued outcomes for those we served; yet they were rarely achieved. If we continue to adjust our vision with an individualized support lens, we can look downstream in the evolution of developmental disabilities services and watch as definitions of outcomes morph to express what is valuable to the person.

The DD system struggles to find ways to measure outcomes that reflect basic human yearnings, as typical life experiences resist the forms of measurement that the two operative care models demand. The language of outcomes belongs to a system, not to people living their lives. The more our supports focus on a person's lifestyle, numerical measures become the less relevant. How do we measure a close and satisfying relationship or a comfortable home life? We can measure calculate the hours John attends a work center, or the number of face-to-face units delivered to Harry, but how do we account for Linda and Bernie's life together as a married couple? Quality in life is often revealed in artistic expressions: poems, music, and pictures as opposed in numbers. As support moves to Integrated and Community Model stages, accountability for outcomes is shared and realized through dialogue and shared action.

Gaps Between Our Espoused Values and Our Actions

From the late 1980s into the 1990s, we who led R-Arc sensed the gap between our espoused values and our operating behavior. Around this time we began using practices that invited "the whole system into the room" to create a shared vision about building a more integrated community, one that worked toward citizenship for individuals. The planning method we used was the Future Search Conference, originally developed by Eric Trist and Fred Emery and later popularized by Marvin Weisbord.[29] In essence, the Future Search Method is a learning laboratory designed to percolate creativity and discovery to find common ground related to a future possibility. For us, it was an opportunity to get a cross-section of our agency together with individuals and their families, interested community members and representatives from local and state government to create a vision of desired future. Our intent was to find a way to get the kind of outcomes we seek in our own lives for the individuals served in our legacy services. One exercise of the planning day was particularly effective in opening our perception about what is possible for a person with a developmental disability. It was called *A Letter from the Future*. This exercise asked planning participants to write a letter from the future. The letter was to imagine a person with a developmental disability enjoying a rich life. Here are a few letters from that exercise.

Letters from the Future

Dear Mom,

I know you remember the hurt and pain I felt when I discovered Emily was different from the other children in the neighborhood. Her ongoing struggles to fit in at school and the playground made me believe that a special placement at a residential school would be necessary to keep her safe and comfortable, with others just like her. I guess that's the nature of a protective sister, but how wrong was I?

Emily is now married and living with the man she loves, which warms me, and we are able to talk about our relationships like sisters do. As you know, they started out together in an R-Arc supervised apartment, where they received around-the-clock support. What you don't know is that it became quickly apparent that John and Emily didn't need all that support, and they ended up becoming annoyed and frustrated by staff and landlord intrusions. They really did not appreciate being told what to do, just like you, I or any other adult would feel. In addition to not liking the location of R – Arc leased apartment, they also received ongoing complaints about their dogs. Fortunately, I am happy to write, R-Arc employees were receptive and willing to help them explore other living options. We were all surprised that these options went far beyond the R-Arc program sites and included the possibility of John and Emily owning their own home. What a leap from the playground years ago when I didn't think Emily could handle sticking up for herself!

Well, guess what? It's been two years and they have recently moved into a home that they own. They managed to benefit from a government aid program called "home of your own," which provided enough subsidy to make the purchase reasonable and in their price range. Emily has a job in food service and John works in maintenance at a local school. With their earnings, they have enough to pay the mortgage and to live comfortably. They still get support from R-Arc staff, but on their own terms. It inspires me to examine my own desires in life more, and how I can make my dreams a reality.

Their home has turned into a wonderful sanctuary for their pets and friends. For their dogs, the fenced in backyard has become a place to freely

*romp and relax. For their friends, weekend and holiday get-togethers are
a time to look forward to eat well and play table games with people they
love. This, and their involvement in the local church, has really connected
Emily and John to a community that they never experienced when they
were growing up. There are times when Joe and I come home from a Sunday
dinner over at John and Emily's and I believe the painful world of Emily's
childhood is completely washed away with these new times. I'm so thrilled
to share this with you. It's been an amazing journey to watch unfold. Thank
you for reading this Mom.*

Your daughter,
Jane

Dear Mr. Meissner,

*I think it's important for you to hear a message from the future about what
is possible for Richard in 2006. I know it is difficult for you to imagine Richard in anything but a highly supervised program environment, given his history of intense behavioral outbursts, and I can understand this viewpoint.
However, I also appreciate that R-Arc has stood by Richard after he bombed
out of each residence the agency placed him in. I also know how challenging
it is to keep him safe (and the community safe) when he constantly gets into
altercations with others in his neighborhood. It will take some risks and
fearlessness to continue to reshape Richard's supports to help him find his
path and calling, but it will be worth the work.*

*Imagine this. It is 2006 and all of that has dramatically changed. After all
those 24/7 support arrangements on pins and needles, Richard now lives
in his own supported apartment with staff living close by to give him assistance only when he needs it, without getting in his face which, as you know,
doesn't really work for our strong-willed friend Richard. The apartment is
located in a neighborhood that has a very active street, and Richard loves to
socialize. His routine consists of walking the blocks and stopping to converse
with all the people sitting on their stoops. Well known and liked by all, even
the police now support Richard, understanding how to deescalate him when
he is agitated. He makes it quite clear this is his neighborhood and this is
where he wants to stay, feeling great ownership of the life he has developed
in this community. It truly is his home. Even when the Director of Residential Services suggested an apartment in a "better neighborhood," Richard
responded with an emphatic no!*

*As if built just for Richard, the apartment has some great land space where
he can store all his collectables (which used to be a big problem at a certified
residence) and grow a blossoming vegetable garden. His ripe, red tomatoes
have been a big hit and he loves to share them with his willing neighbors.
This practice in cultivating gardening skills have grown into a lawn mowing*

business which he operates in his neighborhood to a steady, and reliable clientelle.

You may be thinking that Richard needs a restrictive residential program with behavioral supports, but trust me it's the future now, where a small shift in perspective and placement can make a big impact. 2006, and Rich is decidedly his own man.

Respectfully,

Harold, DSP

Dear Arc,

I would like to share a story about my daughter Giovanna and Lydia, a classmate in her 4th grade class. Lydia wrote a story about herself and Giovanna for Mrs. Wendall's weekly class project titled, "You Gotta Have Heart," telling the teacher that she wanted to do something for a girl in her church group named Giovanna that has a problem with her brain. She wanted to help Giovanna with her school work, as she can't memorize more than five words at a time. This act of kindness turned into a friendship between my daughter and Lydia. Her story follows:

When I got to Awana Club, Giovanna had a friend with her. I gave a note to Giovanna at small group in a blue envelope that I made myself. When I gave the letter to her, she opened the envelope and read it. My letter said: "Dear Giovanna, God loves you and so do we. Thank you for coming to Awana Club at our church with us. You are very smart and you are fun to play with. –Lydia."

Her friend asked if she could read it. Giovanna said, "no," and that was all she said. But there was a nonstop smile on her face for the rest of the day that told me she liked her card. I felt very good when I gave her the note. There was somebody in the world that could be my friend. I have made Giovanna my buddy. I help her with memorizing verses at game time. I cheer for her when she gets awards in group time, and best of all we know that we are always there for each other. Giovanna has made a big difference in my life. I am thankful for her.

After reading Lydia's story, I realized that Giovanna could have real friends and a full life, just like the rest of us. As a parent, much like Lydia's note to Giovanna, this is my gift. I too, have had a smile on my face, non-stop.

Sincerely,

Giovanna's Mom

In narrative form, these letters illuminate aspects of life in the way a poem transforms the mundane into gifted moments. These small but joyful gifts emanate from the core of the human experience, as defined by our choices, our relationships, our contributions, and the life space that we inhabit. As a service provider we speak about outcomes as opposed to life experiences, because it is expected that our actions and efforts will lead to something measurable in institutional or managed care terms. But these letters remind us that for people, it is simply about living, not achieving service defined outcomes.

In the Institutional and Managed Care Models, real-life outcomes exist in service documents but are not supported by the way services are organized and managed. Watching what is enacted within these service models tells us it is more about placement, compliance, treatment and managing resources efficiently. All these outcomes have their value to the system, yet they are not about person-centered, life enhancing experiences. Valued outcomes as defined by John O'Brien (1988) are achieved through self-directed actions on the part of individuals, families, and natural communities, not through delegation to a service provider. Service providers can assist in the process through the provision of supports, but not simply by handing off responsibility for the work to others.

Valued Experiences and Accomplishments

John O'Brien provides a clear presentation of the connection between core life engagements and human service outcomes in this diagram.[30]

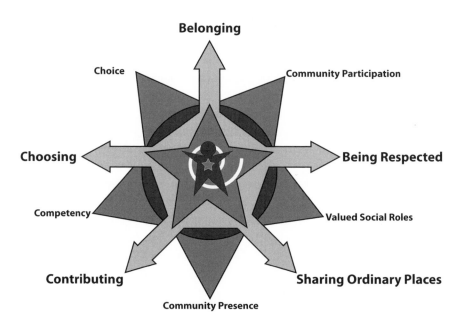

This diagram depicts experiences and accomplishments reflecting basic human yearnings, and the elements that need to be present for a person with a disability to function as a citizen, socially and legally. They are antidotes to marginalization experienced by people with developmental disabilities. Shut out and isolated from community, restricted in personal choice making, demeaned and made invisible, individuals with developmental disabilities assumed diminished status in the general community. The valued outcomes are the pathway out of social exclusion.

Connecting Valued Outcomes to Individualized Supports

These valued life experiences are the focus when designing supports in the Integrated Supports and Community Supports Models. They identify belonging to community and association, choosing one's life style and living conditions, finding ways to contribute vocationally or otherwise, developing self and sharing ordinary places with friends and family as valued priorities. O'Brien's framework guides the effort to individualize services. Without supporting valued experiences, individualizing supports is merely a hollow exercise that sacrifices the positive possibilities in the Integrated and Community Supports stages of evolution. Supporting valued human experiences is at the core of R-Arc's mission and purpose. Four aspirations of individualized supports development have been succinctly named: work, friends, health and home. These are human elements that would be universally considered in the quest for a meaningful life, all realized with choice. The following graphic, borrowed from Beth Mount, articulates an agenda for providers for individualizing supports.

Work	Friends
I am increasing my wage earning capacity via:	**I am growing & deepening relationships with:**
• a paid job	• family, friends & intimate partners
• an internship or volunteer job where I am learning new skills	• neighbors & neighborhood life, co-workers & colleagues
• attending college or other education program & working on campus	• associations, civic & volunteer organizations
• my own small business	• self-advocacy & support groups
• a career in music, art, photography or other creative work	
I am developing my body, mind & spirit via:	**I live in my own home with:**
• physical fitness & nutrition	• my family & supports as needed
• routine & reliable medical & dental care	• a support circle & self-directed supports as needed
• psychological health & support to communicate	• a roommate who shares my home & my life
• spiritual life & restoration	• someone who lives upstairs, next door or in the neighborhood who provides support when needed
• other personal routines that are good for me	• support staff who are present all or most of the time
Health	**Home**

Key Points

- Valued outcomes are ones that have to do with what is meaningful in life to an individual. What is meaningful varies with each person though often involves relationships, vocation, spirituality, home, connection, and contribution to a community.

- Each care and support model is wired to help bring forth certain outcomes. The valued outcomes described above are difficult to measure and realize in care models but can blossom with the appropriate supports as seen in the Integrated and Community Supports Models.

- Service providers can increase the chances of an individual getting to a valued outcome by working on the four aspirations of individualized supports development –work, friends, health and home.

Guided Self or Team Learning Journey

1. What outcomes are being worked on with the individuals supported by your agency? Are these system-outcomes, consumer-outcomes, or citizen-based outcomes? Is there a gap between written or stated outcomes and what actually happens in your service environments?

2. At a time when most agencies straddle two or more care/support models, there are increasing expectations from government or payers of services to "measure outcomes," that are different in each care/support model. How might your agency reconcile this requirement with difficulty of measuring authentic valued outcomes? What methods work? Which are misaligned?

3. Consider interviewing a person who receives services from your agency: Ask the individual about what is working in her life now in terms of relationship, home, and work. Then ask what she would like to change, what would she like to have more of or less of in these life areas. Lastly, ask how you or the agency could support changes or improvements in her life.

4. Host an open dialogue session with individuals and families about life outcomes they value. Consider having individuals and families write a letter from the future that reflects valued outcomes playing out their lives on an everyday basis. Give people creative license to express a positive image of the future in a letter, in a picture, skit, or poem. Note the themes.

6

Competing Commitments and the Dynamics of Being Stuck

Have a dialogue between the two opposing parts and you will find that they always start out fighting each other until we come to an appreciation of difference, ... a oneness and integration of the two opposing forces. Then the civil war is finished, and your energies are ready for your struggle with the world. [31]

—*Fritz Perls*

Not being able to change doesn't mean we're lazy, stubborn, or weak. [32]
—*Robert Kegan and Lisa Laskow Lahey*

I could see him ahead of me working steadily upward, pausing now and then to take bearing. My progress was ludicrously slow. Every inch I gained in attitude was an effort... I struggled on – why I do not know. [33]
—*Charlie Houston*

My friends and family know that I am a passionate hiker and enjoy striking out on my own on a mountain adventure, where no trails exist. Bushwhacking requires capacities and skills that both transcend and include those of the trail hiker. A foray into uncharted territory exponentially increases the complexity of the adventure. While a marked nature trail may require consideration of a few details to coordinate, a trek into unmarked territory is unpredictable and demands a series of adjustments based on learning in the field. It also means considering balancing the risks of getting lost or hurt with the excitement of an intimate and unique hiking experience. Typically, trail hikers benefit from those who traveled the paths before them, and whose efforts are often documented in trail guides with routes plotted on maps. Bushwhackers rely

---

* In 1953 Houston participated in a courageous, if failed, rescue attempt when he and his fellow mountain climbers turned back on K2. They tried to save the life of their climbing partner by lowering him progressively down the mountain despite the altitude, despite the storm and the danger of avalanches, despite their complete exhaustion and despite the ensuing accident that nearly killed them all.

on their orienting skills, intuitive senses, and tolerance for difficult and unforgiving terrain. They have but a vision of the destination, yet they enjoy the adventure and are willing and able to change their route on a moment's notice given field information. Bushwhacking is about discovery as opposed to the predictive quality of trail hiking. When trail hikers get stuck, they consult a trail guide. When bushwhackers get disoriented, they seek a vantage point from which the contour of the field can be seen. The evolutionary journey from Institutional Care to Integrated and Community Supports is more like bushwhacking than trail hiking. In this chapter, I explore the nature of change we are facing as we evolve to Integrated and Community Supports and the challenges we need to address when caught by the competing commitments experienced anytime a shift to another stage occurs.

Reasons for Being Stuck

For our agency, the challenge is to make progress on individualized supports within the context of our legacy services. We often claim, in the process of prototyping a new support arrangement, "we really mean it this time." We often find ourselves in a backwash of competing commitments: we are obligated to operate an ongoing legacy concern, and are also passionate about our edge work with individuals and families. It is no surprise that many of us who operate legacy programs are feeling stuck in our genuine interest to move to individualized supports. Other than the weight of our legacy service baggage, we get stuck for three main reasons: underestimating the complexity of the change we are facing, being unaware of our underlying beliefs about people with disabilities, and incorrectly (or inadequately) responding to our change challenge. By miscoding the nature and depth of change that is required, we fail to develop the readiness and resources to be successful. As the bushwhacking metaphor suggests, it is critical to find a vantage point that reveals the competing commitments operating in our world so that we can generate adaptive strategies. This entails testing assumptions that operate as "truths" under the Institutional and Managed Care Models. Like the bushwhacker, people, organizations, and systems must test their assumptions about the terrain without exposing themselves to undue jeopardy. We have to challenge current operating norms and beliefs without undermining current support arrangements, or organizational survival. It is worthwhile to stray from the marked trail; a standardized course of travel forgoes the unsurpassed beauty of the deep wilderness.

Legacy Services are a Gift to the Next Generation of Supports

As I have mentioned, the term legacy refers to a gift or a resource that has been handed down by a predecessor to a new generation. As each support paradigm solves the problems of its generation, it also positions the DD field for future innovations. Yet the legacy of our current services continues to shoulder the lion's share of supporting people in community settings (see the Table below). Our ability to evolve our services relies on transcending yet including the best of our current service model.

	Individualized Supports		Group Services	
	% People Served	% Program Budget	%People Served	% Program Budget
Housing	64%	60%	36%	40%
Day Service & Supports	36%	25%	64%	75%
Family Support	35%	42%	65%	58%

The evolutionary process I am suggesting involves growing our capacities to engage in co-designing individualized supports, not in destroying the current service form. I have often felt that engaging in transformational change while functioning as a legacy agency is like changing the tires on a car while driving sixty miles per hour. The change imperative requires that agencies, such as R-Arc, must substantially apply individualized supports while continuing to operate within an Institutional and/or Managed Care system with all of its resource constraints and regulatory trappings. How does an organization manage in times like these?

Scoping Out the Change Territory

Scoping out the geography prior to a bushwhacking adventure is critical to safely and effectively navigate the terrain. With a sense of the terrain, the bushwhacker can anticipate the potential hazards and challenges of unknown woods. These days every change initiative seems to be labeled as transformative, yet the strategies employed seem to fit trail hiking in a predictable and stable environment far better than exploring unmapped territory. Evolving from Managed Care to Integrative Supports is anything but predictable. We are in an experimental phase, testing out structural forms and support practices to realize the sensibility of the Integrative Supports Model.

Simply tagging our change efforts as transformative did not give R-Arc the leverage needed to individualize supports. Instead, perceiving the type and extent of the change we were undertaking helped us to climb out of the quagmire and resume the journey on firmer ground. [34]

Three Types of Change

Ackerman-Anderson[35] describe three types of change: developmental change, transitional change, and transformational change. Each type of change requires different capacities and responses from all key stakeholders.

A woods outing typically involves reading the description of the hike in a guide, preparing for the level of difficulty of the trail, and following the trail markers to your destination. This is the sensibility of developmental change. Service organizations engaged in developmental changes might offer a new vocational service, open a residence for a specialized population (e.g., for people with Prader-Willie syndrome) or implement a consumer software program. The relevant change tools include process improvement tools, continuous quality improvement, conflict resolution, role clarification, team building, and staff training and development programs. This type of change identifies a gap between expectation and performance, articulates an improvement objective, and apples a problem-solving strategy to achieve the objective. Developmental change tools and strategies usually work to improve existing skills, processes, and structures.

When trails erode they must be re-routed and cut to a new destination. This reflects a transitional change sensibility. Transitional changes involve differentiating a new state from an old state, with a link that involves "retooling" the system and its practices to fit the new model. Mergers, consolidations, reorganizations, revising systemic financial payment structures (such as moving from fee for service to capitation payments,) re-engineering and/or creating new services, processes, systems and products to replace the traditional one are each transitional changes. The Medicaid Home-and-Community-Based Waiver[36] implemented across the US in the 1980s and 1990s reflected this type of change in the developmental disabilities field. Strategic planning, project management, setting goals and objectives with timelines, developing metrics, and designing new business models are expressions of this type of change. Transitional change is closest to the current energy around re-engineering institutional service forms to managed care. Transitional change, like developmental change, does not seem to reflect the kind of evolutionary shifts that occur when relationships between provider and recipient are realigned to partnerships.

TRANSITIONAL CHANGE

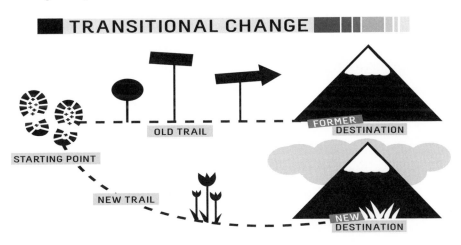

First ascents of mountains in uncharted and rugged territory are transformational experiences. The intention to climb some of the highest and most remote mountains in the world has been compared to the quest for the Holy Grail. Transformational change, the most complex form of change, involves fundamental reordering of thinking, beliefs, culture, relationships, and behavior. Moving into the Integrative Supports stage requires a change approach that turns assumptions inside out and disrupts familiar rituals and structures. It rejects command and control relationships in favor of co-creative partnerships.

TRANSFORMATIONAL CHANGE

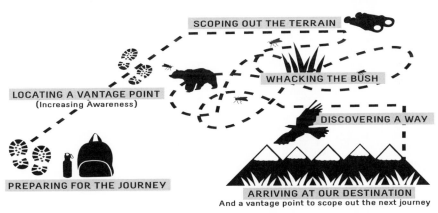

Disappointment is inevitable when people seek a result that calls for transformational change with the understanding and social architecture suited to developmental change or transitional change –as many DD systems are doing under the heading of "system transformation." Coloring a transitional change initiative with transformational language only increases confusion, and risks setting up double binds by pitting the requirements of the established support model against the effort to create Integrative Supports.

Responding to Change

Moving to the next stage requires new thinking and acting which can only develop if we avoid quick-fix reactions and adherence to routine problem solving processes. Otto Scharmer explores the dynamics of innovation with Theory U. Scharmer proposes that intractably stuck problems require breaking patterned practices of the past through innovative processes.[37] In our journey, this involves identifying our subconscious presumptions to disengage them. Once this is achieved, we can enter an enlightened, collaborative process: listening to alternative views without passing judgment, welcoming new concepts without cynicism, and sensing purpose more deeply along with trying on different practices, roles, and relationships without fear of losing a sense of ourselves. We have a conversation about the scope of loss we are mutually willing to risk. Performing these shifts in understanding, experiencing, and focus, prepare us to experiment with the agreed upon limits.

Clearly, being routinely reactive to events does not orient an agency to engage in transformational change. And redesigning process and structure has not had much success in getting personal outcomes of value for people. Sitting in a legacy agency attempting individualized supports at a self-directed, co-designed level requires a new approach that is flexible to circumstance, molded by our deepest intentions and creativity. This table illustrates different types of change responses and which problem level they address.

FOUR LEVELS OF RESPONDING TO CHANGE

LEVEL ONE	ROUTINE PROBLEMS	REACTING TO EVENTS WITH QUICK FIXES
LEVEL TWO	DEVELOPMENTAL PROBLEMS	REDESIGNING POLICIES
LEVEL THREE	TRANSITIONAL PROBLEMS	REFRAMING: VALUES AND ASSUMPTIONS
LEVEL FOUR	TRANSFORMATIONAL PROBLEMS	REGENERATING: SOURCES OF ENERGY

Surfacing Assumptions and Beliefs

There is nothing like operating from a top-down position to ignite opposition. R-Arc learned this when we attempted to "downsize" our sheltered workshop. We were motivated by our passion for the right of all people to be included in their communities. For us, this meant closing our segregated group settings and helping people get employment in the community. As value-based and wonderfully progressive this was in the late 1980's, our efforts were met with considerable resistance from some individuals attending our work center and their families. Our interest to downsize the workshop floundered when we got stuck in a bubble of our own assumptions and neglected to engage others who saw the world differently. This was my first wake-up call that others essential to enlist in the change may view the world through a different lens and weigh the risks and rewards of change differently. From our vantage point we saw vistas of an inclusive society that others did not. Looking back, I see how unilateral and arbitrary our process was and how we neglected our relationships with the very people we sincerely wanted to benefit from our change objective. In our effort to make things better, we created considerable anxiety in others. We had not considered that operating from a position of authority and expertise was out of sync with our desire to promote inclusion. The resistance we encountered gave us pause and an opportunity to examine our approach to change. It is now clear to me that we needed to increase our awareness of our intentions and the transparency of our process before we could truly engage people and families in transformational change.

The Ladder of Inference – Seeing Our Assumptions

At this point in our journey, we were fortunate to be exposed to the concepts of the Learning Organization through the work of Chris Argyris and Peter Senge.[38] We were attracted to the affirmative, humanistic orientation of the learning organization which emphasized an intelligent systems perspective coupled with self-development, team learning strategies, dialogic processes, and a heightened awareness of how one's world view (labeled Mental Model) influences structural design and behavior. The learning organization approach was complete with tools to promote reflective practice, including Chris Argyris's "Ladder of Inference." This framework depicts a mostly internal process by which we move from observed experience to perceptual selection to thought (assumption making and conclusions) to action. This process often occurs rapidly, and beneath our awareness.

Given all the stimuli in our world, there is a practical need to filter out some of it to avoid becoming completely saturated and ineffective. Through a filtering process, we select certain data as a way to focus our attention. Our understanding of the selected data and choosing actions to implement the meaning we make of the world is strongly influenced by our background and cultural frame of reference. This process becomes routine for purposes of efficiency, and of course, can have both negative and positive results. Thinking and sense-making is what makes us human and functionally effective in our everyday world, however, by selecting some things and not others on which to focus, we by definition leave out other aspects of the world. This exposes us to errors in perception and reasoning, leading to flawed assumptions, decisions and actions. Without checking and challenging our data and assumptions with others, we can make misinformed decisions, perpetuate dysfunctional routines, and ultimately get into protracted conflicts with others. We also end up applying the same old interpretations and solutions to stuck situations, failing to find new and innovative ways to solve complex problems such as moving to a more evolved support model. Otto Scharmer labels acting on a pre-set of perceptions and assumptions as "downloading." We humbly saw this reflected in our unsuccessful attempt to close our work center.

The Ladder of Inference can be applied as a reflective tool for understanding and sharing one's reasoning with others, both as a way to be more completely understood, and as a way to challenge the adequacy of one's thinking prior to implementing a decision. This helped us to more deeply listen to and understand the individuals and families that opposed the work center closure. It also helped clarify our position. Typically, this process reveals the values embedded in opposing positions. By listening and seeing other viewpoints, we disrupted our typical patterns of downloading.

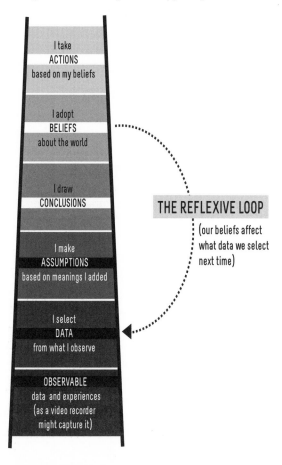

I take actions based on my beliefs	**Place people in specialized programs and protective environments.**	**Support people in integrated settings in the community.**
I adopt beliefs about the world	The world treats people who are different negatively.	The world is a more positive place when it embraces the principles of diversity and inclusion.
I draw conclusions	Therefore, we need to develop specialized and separate developmental programs and interventions.	Therefore, people need to be supported in person centered ways that promote community membership.
I make assumptions based on the meanings I added	People with disabilities are vulnerable in the community and need separate and special environments to live safety.	People with disabilities can live in the community with supports. Natural friendships and families are what keep people safe and promote personal growth.
I add meanings (cultural and personal)	People with disabilities don't fit in with the mainstream based on their abnormalities.	All people have human rights and are part of the community based on their human qualities.
I select "data" from what I observe	Focus on the needs, dysfunctions, and deficiencies of individuals.	Focus on the capacities and interests of individuals.
Observable "data" and experiences	People with developmental disabilities have difficulty learning and adapting in life areas such as home living, leisure, and work. They have the same human needs, interests, and motivations of people without developmental disabilities. They also have some capacities to have friends, work, and grow.	People with developmental disabilities have difficulty learning and adapting in life areas such as home living, leisure, and work They have the same human needs, interests, and motivations of people without developmental disabilities. They also have some capacities to have friends, work, and grow.

Discovering and Appreciating Opposing Views of the World

We applied the Ladder of Inference to better understand the stuck position we were in with individuals and families who valued the sheltered workshop and were opposed to closing its doors. We discovered that the opposing viewpoints, as depicted above, revealed different world views expressing real tensions present in our social field. We came to acknowledge and work with these differences because they reflected different aspects of our reality. This helped us assume more respectful relationships with families and individuals, seeing more clearly the competing positions and interests that were operating in our world. With increased understanding of our differences and our intention to engage in a dialogue with others, we focused on appreciating varying viewpoints instead of assuming we are right and they are wrong. As a result, we sought to collaborate with families and individuals. This, in turn, resulted in a modification of our strategy. We altered our goal from closing two work centers to downsizing the census by 50% and freezing new entrants into the program. We also prototyped one of New York State's first inclusive and individualized day programs based in community settings instead of a program site (in our state's jargon this is now called "day habilitation without walls"). Using the ladder of inference to reveal competing world views helped us see things from a systems perspective with more of the elements fully revealed. This allowed us to be more nuanced and strategic in our change process. In hindsight, we avoided the mistake of "hopping over" a current service practice by finding ways to build social (relational) bridges to the next support model.

Immunity to Change

As we continued to push through the tangle of operational concerns of our legacy agency, slogging our way toward Integrated and Community Supports, we were losing our energy and becoming stressed about not making progress on our individualized supports agenda. Judgment and cynicism started to rear their heads. Fears about being incompetent, losing control, being lazy and comfortable with status quo, or just plain arrogant about already being person-centered, swirled in our heads. Fortunately, we discovered Robert Kegan's and Lisa Laskow-Lahey's book, *Immunity to Change, How to Overcome it and Unlock the Potential in Yourself and your Organization*.[39] The authors helped us to understand how the typical reasons for organizations being stuck fell short of explaining our situation and gave us a different way to make sense of our reality.

When one experiences immunity to change, the premise is that there is a hidden dynamic that is holding the change effort hostage. There are three dimensions of immunity. First, we do things that work against the change we desire to make. These actions are tied to the commitments we have made to ourselves and others that contradict or distract from our stated interest in change. Second, if it is not managed well, the anxiety a change initiative produces can deplete our energy and disable our motivation to work for the desired change. Third, simply not seeing the dynamics of our situation can render any change strategy ineffective. For example, we may have the goal to support people in their own apartment, but currently structure our resources and staffing around group homes. In our interest to individualize supports, we may be simultaneously committed to assist a person to be more autonomous while addressing their safety by having complete control and oversight of the service location to avoid risks of liability and regulatory compliance.

For us in the DD field, all this has to do with operating in an increasingly complex environment replete with competing commitments. As the ladder of inference displays the underlying beliefs and assumptions that propel our actions, uncovering our competing commitments reveals the dynamics of the system that binds us and locates a way to leverage change.

Our Competing Commitments

Competing commitments can be unpacked on the Immunity to Change chart developed by Kegan and Lahey. The four-column chart is designed to display the dynamics of our stuckness. The first column contains our goals related to our passion to individualize supports and assisting people to get a life of their own choosing. The second column lists what we do that encourages or discourages movement towards that goal. The third column identifies the goals and objectives that compete against individualizing supports that exist within our agency and the relevant regulatory environment. The last column identifies the assumptions that make it difficult to actualize our good intentions. These assumptions operate at the individual, team, organizational and systems levels.

Completing the chart abridged on the next page at a strategy retreat showed us the system we are in and the assumptions we need to challenge to break free. As with the ladder of inference, once we surface and examine our assumptions, we can see where they fall short in describing reality. We can test our assumptions by inquiring about their applicability, relevancy, and completeness, or by running small, innovative experiments to challenge their adequacy.

Pitting Safety Against Self-Direction

Reflecting on the completed chart, our management team noticed dominant themes. The most obvious theme characterized a polarized context, both internal and external to the agency. It involved pitting "keeping people safe" against a strong emerging energy around self-determination. Being safe and being self-directed are not mutually exclusive, given that most of us desire to work and live in safe places but take risks to grow personally. However, due to our field's institutional history and the nearly exclusive emphasis on people's vulnerability that motivates much policy and practice, we work in a force field of opposing tensions in which our commitment to supporting self-determination is easily overpowered by risk aversion. This is primarily caused by our beliefs about people with disabilities and the role we assume in relationship to these beliefs. So intense is the rulemaking around keeping individuals safe, that we end up short-circuiting our capacity to support a person to be self-directed. As policy makers at State and Federal levels move to reform the DD service system, their rhetoric heats up around person-centered planning and individualized supports while simultaneously generating reams of restrictive safety regulations enforced through hierarchical structures.

Stated Commitments	What We Are Doing or Not Doing That Keeps Our Stated Commitments from Being Fully Realized	Competing Commitments	Our Big Assumptions
We are committed to to creating organizational conditions which facilitate the development of individualized supports.	A large percentage of our resources are generated by & support group settings.	• We are committed to the financial stability of our organization in the light of potentially disruptive change. • We structure our services to fit regulations & funding models.	We need to continue to operate our group options for fiscal sustainability, choice, & maintenance of a viable support option for individuals will multiple disabilities.
We are committed to realigning our relationships with individuals & families to partnership & shared power.	We spent a significant amount of time meeting documentation, compliance & administrative requirements.	We are committed to buffering our agency against negative government audits. Our roles relating to fiscal control & related human resource management practices are essential to compliance with legal & regulatory requirements.	Most of the time of R-Arc Administration will be spent in meeting the growing work load generated as a result of more regulation leaving few hours for organization development work.
We are committed to assisting individuals with developmental disabilities realize valued roles in the community & obtain citizenship status.	Most of our staffing patterns are arranged to support group programs.	We are committed to supporting the wishes of families & individuals who like their group placements.	We are the experts on human resource & financial management. If we share decision making with individuals & families, we will lose control, increase legal actions & budgets will fail. The community is largely unprepared & under-resourced to support individuals with disabilities. It is not accepting of individuals with disabilities.

While this certainly illustrates our double bind, the tensions reveal there is an important conversation happening. It also points out that the shift from an institutional model to a more evolved support model is in play. No longer is R-Arc or the larger DD field sitting squarely and comfortably in the institutional legacy service model. We are certainly in transition to managed care and possibly entering the parameter of a support model. As we know in our personal lives, development to a more evolved support orientation can be arrested when our assumptions remain hidden and untested and we hold on to status quo or roles we are comfortable with even in the face of change.

Transformational change is not clear, there are no shortcuts. Commitments often of equal value are operating against each other, illustrating the classic force field that suspends a social system in equilibrium. Equilibrium is not a bad thing, unless it preserves status quo to the detriment of a devalued population. Before we can fully situate in a supports model, things will be messy with only patches of coherency, similar to the experience of making a mid-life career change or finding a new sense of self after the loss of a spouse.

The Power of a New Vantage Point

The second aspect of the dynamic of stuckness is illustrated by an experience I had with a bushwhacking trip in the Adirondacks. A map of the Jay Wilderness Area identifies Natural Dam and over the past few years I had made four attempts to find it without luck. On the fifth attempt I arrived at a position on a ridge where I noticed a large drop in the forest floor. It dawned on me that, from the perspective one gets from an airplane, the area surrounding where I was standing would look topographically like a dam. From this vantage point, I saw my errors in perception, and my destination came into full view. From that moment on I knew exactly where the Natural Dam was and how to get to it.

Testing our Big Assumptions

The Immunity to Change Map affords us a view of the big assumptions that hold us in status quo. Kegan and Lahey talk about designing tests or experiments to challenge our big assumptions and overcome our inertia. R-Arc did exactly this when we initiated a series of actions over the years to test assumptions about the way people were supported residentially. Early in our history we successfully challenged the notion that everyone in a community residence had to share a bedroom with at least one roommate, a requirement that most adults in the United States don't meet without choice. The big assumptions supporting doubling up were both social and fiscal. It was taken for granted that residents had roommates like students in college dorms and that single rooms would be unaffordable for agencies. Since the mid-1980s everyone supported residentially by R-Arc has their own bedroom. This does not seem like such a big deal now, but back in the 1980s this was unheard of in New York State.

Another big assumption about residential support was that people with severe intellectual and physical disabilities needed to be served in Intermediate Care Facilities (ICF), a medical model setting. We challenged this notion, successfully supporting people with the same clinical profile as those placed in ICF's by adapting the supports to meet their needs in a less restrictive community residence. By bringing in clinical supports only when they were needed as opposed to prescriptively built within the ICF, we shed the medical-facility atmosphere from the support environment. This assumption was further tested in the latter 1990s and early 2000s as we began to support people with severe and multiple disabilities in individually adapted apartments. What we learned from these efforts has prepared us to support people who would otherwise live out their final days in a nursing home to stay in the comfort of their own home. Our tests got a bit more daring when we challenged the whole concept of group living by dismantling a community residence and using the resources to develop individualized living arrangements. All sorts of assumptions (e.g., individual safety, socialization, cost efficiency, and site management) were tested in the process of redesigning living environments from group to individual through processes of restructuring and reinvesting resources. While at times we discovered that a piece of our big assumption was accurate (and we had adjusted our strategy accordingly,) much of it fell under the weight of new evidence derived from our "tests."

First Step out of Stuckness

To take the first step out of stuckness, we must have a clear view of our gridlocked condition and the nature of change we have invoked. By running experiments of calculable risk to test the validity of the assumptions we have that tie us to the status quo and initiating ongoing loops of innovative prototypes, we may be led to the next generation of supports. The following chapters describe the many paths R–Arc took to release the bind of our competing commitments.

Key Points

- Moving from legacy services to individualized supports is truly transformational. Implementing change at this level requires shifts in thinking and behaving, and a realignment of power and influence in the support relationship. This is prerequisite to redesigning services and supports and their accompanying structures and resources.

- There are many ways to stall a change process, none more powerful than the competing commitments that hold us to status quo. Understanding this dynamic is an important lever to pull in moving a change effort forward.

- Discovering the diversity of perspectives and assumptions about people with developmental disabilities and their capacities helps to find common ground for a change effort to move forward as opposed to staying locked in combat with families, providers, government agencies, and community members when attempting to transform legacy services.

Guided Self or Team Learning Journey

1. Is your agency committed to individualizing supports and citizen outcomes? If so, how does your leadership define the nature of change (i.e., developmental, transitional, transformative) related to individualizing supports? At what level are you and your agency responding to the call for change?

2. Using *Exercise 5: The Ladder of Inference* (page 165), discover the assumptions, interpretations, and conclusions you and others have, and the actions you and others take related to legacy services and individualizing supports.

3. What are the competing commitments that stall your agency's change efforts to move to individualizing supports? Complete a competing commitments chart for your agency (*Exercise 6* on page 167).

FRIENDS AND MENTORS ON THE HEROES JOURNEY: HANNS MEISSNER STANDING WITH
SANDY VAN ECK (BEHIND HIM), BETH MOUNT AND HENRIETTA MESSIER.

7

Preparing for the Journey
Self as An Instrument of Change

People with a high level of personal mastery live in a continual learning mode. They never "arrive." Sometimes, language, such as the term "personal mastery'" creates a misleading sense of definiteness, of black and white. But personal mastery is not something you possess. It is a process. It is a lifelong discipline. People with a high level of personal mastery are acutely aware of their ignorance, their incompetence, their growth areas. And they are deeply self-confident. Paradoxical? Only for those who do not see the that the journey is the reward.[40]

—*Peter Senge*

The nature, quality and amount of change that you want to see in the world is directly relative to the nature, quality and amount of change that you are ready to go through inside yourself.[41]

—*Tim Merry*

To produce the creative support arrangements critical to realizing a full life for people with developmental disabilities, organizational leaders must intentionally create blue space for social innovation. This process begins with leaders expanding their individual personal capacities to develop good form. Acting as an instrument of change is compatible to Gestalt's concept of "presence," which entails the effective integration of deep personal purposes with self awareness, well developed competencies, and a living commitment to lifelong learning.[42] This type of leadership evolution is self-managed; it integrates personal vision with intentional action and ongoing deep reflection to gain a greater understanding of one's impact on others and effectiveness in a situation. My first step out of the gridlock of competing commitments was to become more aware of the patterns of assumptions and actions that held our agency in status quo and my own contribution to this dynamic.

The Hero's Journey

Each one of us are the most powerful tool to create blue space in our organizations. Although I have made this journey as someone holding formal positions of authority, leadership can emanate from any place in a social field. Effective leaders of social change and innovative practice, wherever and whenever they surface, hear a calling to participate in a change process. In responding to their calling, these leaders find themselves on a journey into uncharted territory. This journey is a deeply felt personal experience of contending with foreign world views, new expectations, and new challenges often within a context of competing commitments. Joseph Campbell describes this as "the hero's journey." The pattern typical of the hero's journey includes: responding to a calling; letting go of traditional roles, beliefs, and relationships; moving into new perspectives and experiences; and emerging with new insights and practice to benefit the journeyer's community. Otto Scharmer's Theory U process follows the tracks of the archetypal hero's journey in a sequence of movements that result in innovative solutions to today's toughest problems.[43]

THE HERO'S JOURNEY
Engaging the U Process

THE CALLING

BREAKING AWAY FROM ROUTINES

MOVEMENT INTO NEW TERRITORIES

EMERGENCE OF NEW PERSPECTIVE

LETTING GO OF OLD ROLES
and structure. Connecting to deeper purpose.

INTEGRATING INTO PRACTICE

PROTOTYPING NEW SUPPORTS

VISIONING THE NEW

Inspired by Otto Scharmer

My Personal Leadership Journey

The change imperative sparked by the evolution to individualized supports has significantly affected my own maturity as a person and a leader. One of the greatest challenges I have faced in my career is figuring out the form my leadership should take during these transformational times. I started my learning journey at the tail end of one highly disruptive change era – deinstitutionalization – and the emergence of a community – based system – only to become part of another within a decade. Before I could take a breath and gain equilibrium, I found myself at the cusp of an emerging form of support with the advent of self-determination and individualization – a set of practices supporting people already in the process of real living. In retrospect, my response to this transformation has consistently been: create blue space for appreciation and innovation to flourish.

As a formal organizational leader, I am responsible to guide my agency through the rough waters of real transformation. In order to do so, I realize that I need to continually develop my capacity as an instrument of change. This means I must embody the principles and characteristics of an appreciative leader and a reflective practitioner by being present, relentlessly inquisitive, profoundly humble, and authentically engaged in pursuit of good form in my person and in my relationships. Coming from an interest in fostering creative and collaborative workplaces, I reject the command and control model of management. In disregarding all the military and machine metaphors that so often inform management practices, I am opened to embrace an image of an organization as a living community. My vision of organizational life consists of authentic relationships supported by an appreciative culture. I envision R-Arc having a capacity to continuously create social expressions of inclusion within a nurturing and safe environment where everyone's learning is promoted and their contributions are valued.

The call to participate in transforming legacy services is heard and experienced differently from person to person. I come to this work with a strong sense of the injustice heaped upon various peoples throughout history. The root of this inclination, I am sure, is in my experience growing up in the home of a Jewish immigrant and his German war bride. My father barely escaped the terror of the infamous Crystal Night, when Nazi Brown Shirts violated Jewish homes and businesses throughout Germany. Uprooted at the age of nineteen from his home and educational pursuits, my father emigrated to New York City under the sponsorship of a cousin living in the United States. Five years later, he was recruited into General Patton's army, and while on a mission in Germany met his future bride, my mother. The psychology of a life disrupted by war and persecution permeated our household and shaped my world view. I became driven by a strong ethic of social justice, which was reinforced by the social happenings of the 1960s. The civil rights movement and the Vietnam War were of critical importance in formulating my interest to build inclusive communities. The passion of the sixties, for me, exists in Martin Luther King Jr "I Have a Dream" speech. To this day it continues to echo in my mind and brings tears to my eyes. My personality makeup consists of an amalgam of developmental experiences and family dynamics within the context of a sixties culture that sensitized me to the plight of socially marginalized people. I have ended up with a significant need for affiliation coupled with an appreciative frame of reference. You might have noticed, as you have read this book, my attraction to all things that theoretically shine. This makes me simultaneously attracted to emotional and intellectual pursuits; I value ideas in concert with the people that I care about in my life space.

My Calling

Given my affinity to the ethic of social justice, I have enthusiastically accepted the invitation to collaborate with families and individuals to re-order both the work and the social field. However, this calling lay dormant in terms of a career until I volunteered at Essex Arc (now Mountain Lake Services), a provider agency located in the Adirondack Mountains of New York State. Connecting with Joan, a person with developmental disabilities at Essex Arc, drew me into the field of developmental disabilities and provided an outlet to express what was deep inside of me.

This initial calling disrupted my general impressions of and assumptions about individuals with developmental disabilities. Up to that point my contact with people with this label was minimal. As a youth in school, I would catch fleeting glimpses of a few students with disabilities walking down a hallway to a classroom in an undisclosed location on a schedule purposely designed to avoid contact with "typical" students. Other than that, my only other experience with a person with a developmental disability was from a summer job I had at age eighteen. Jimmy had recently moved from Letchworth Village, a large institution located in Rockland County, New York, into an apartment over the garage of a benefactor. Jimmy was described to me as "slow." He was built like a bull, worked hard at the construction site and had a tendency to go to bars, get drunk and then get rolled for his money. I liked Jimmy and enjoyed working with him. He seemed close to "normal" to me, as we could work, joke, and hang out together at the job. Working with Joan at Essex Arc was different. Joan could not speak so she needed to express herself with gestures that, for the uninitiated, were easily misunderstood. Somehow, after a time and without words, I deeply connected with Joan. I eagerly looked forward to my visits with Joan as she did with me. Small gestures –a glance or a faint smile communicated an intuitive understanding between us. Afternoons with Joan slowed time, and I learned how to match her pace, and enjoy the nuanced moments.

My relationship with Joan, which I remember fondly, caused me to rethink what it meant to be human. Up to that point I held a core assumption, which was that verbal exchange is one of the essential qualities of the human experience. I now discovered an alternative language.

Disrupting My Worldview

Joan disrupted my worldview. My typical thoughts and responses were disarmed, and I moved empathically into her world. Afterwards, in my own reflective space at home or perhaps when I was walking in the woods, I became aware of a shift in my attention away from Joan's disability. I began to notice Joan's capacity to enjoy the present moment, and the gift she gave me of opening my world to valuing a person's spirit, versus their assigned roles or achievements. These perceptual shifts were not just regarding Joan, but also about people, with and without developmental disabilities. Looking back at this seminal moment, I see the hero's journey archetype operating underneath. With Joan, I awakened to new possibilities of human experience.

Refocusing my attention away from Joan's disability along with my strong sense of social justice aroused my deepest sense of duty. It was all there, the calling, the breaking away from routine, the movement into different territory, the opening of my heart to another's felt world and the sense of new possibilities to inform everyday experience. Surfacing and testing our often downloaded responses to people is critical in becoming an instrument for change. If this reflective practice is successful, we can visualize a clearer picture of our diverse world and the competing commitments that arrest our personal and organizational development.

A Leadership Developmental Process

Choosing to respond to a deeply felt calling, as I did when I assumed a leadership role in transforming our legacy services into individualized supports, is the first step towards having the capacity to do this kind of work. Significant change journeys take us into uncharted territory in our inner and outer worlds. For organizations, it is a question of culture change; for the individual leader, it's about personal development. The leadership journey tied to this evolutionary pull is experienced as both new and strange. There is no blueprint, no instructional manual or curriculum to build our capacity –it takes inspired commitment and an intuitive venture into the process. Change practitioners must see from a variety of vantage points, favor a creative win/win approach over a competitive win/lose, expand tolerance for risk, become self-aware, and embrace uncertainty. Bottom line: one must trust that our deepest purpose and mission will carry the day.

Developing the self as an instrument of change requires intentional and skillful practice directed at valued contributions to a community. I have identified four stages of leadership development (Bureaucratic, Technician, Change Master and Generative Leader) that are explored in following pages of this chapter and summarized in this table.[44]

Form/Level of Development	Perspective	Authority	Form of Service or Support	Professional/ Individual Relationship
Bureaucratic Leader (operates as a manager in the present system by optimizing current operations & solving problems)	The only perspective the Bureaucrat understands is their own. All other viewpoints are mysterious.	Authority is found in rules & regulations. When two external authorities disagree, it is frustrating but not internally problematic.	Institutional Care (Facility Based & System-Centered)	Bureaucrat, Authoritarian -Patient
Technician/ Problem Solver (operates as a leader by creating strategic direction, scanning for threats & opportunities, motivating people, & communicating performance requirements)	The Technician can take – & become embedded in – the perspectives of other people, theories, & soon. When they see the world, they see it through these other perspectives, & they judge right & wrong, good & bad, from the perspectives of others.	Authority is in an internalized value/principle/ role that comes from outside one's self. When those important values, principles, or roles conflict (as when his religion disagrees with an important value from a partner), the journey person feels an internal tearing, as though parts of himself were pitted against one another.	Managed Care (Service-Based & Administratively Controlled)	Expert-Patient Professional -Consumer

Form/Level of Development	Perspective	Authority	Form of Service or Support	Professional/ Individual Relationship
Change Master (operates as a change manager by facilitating multiple change initiatives, working with resistance, creating & overseeing change management infrastructure & aligning human resources to business change).	The Change Master can take on multiple perspectives while maintaining his own. He can understand the views & opinions of others & often uses these views or opinions to strengthen his/ her own argument or set of principles.	Authority is found in the self. The self-authored system determines the individual's rules & regulations for himself. When others disagree, this can be inconvenient or unpleasant, but is not internally wrenching.	Integrated – Person-Centered Supports & Services	Facilitator/ Broker-Individual
Generative Leader (functions as a change leader through strategies that integrate people, process & content needs including how to change mindset & culture to support new business directions. Also, models self as an instrument of change, catalyzes people's commitment to change, & builds organizational capacity for ongoing change & self-renewal).	The Generative Leader sees & understands the perspectives of others & uses those perspectives to continuously transform this own system, becoming more expansive & more inclusive. He does not use the perspectives of others to fine-tune his own argument or principles like the master does; rather, he puts the entire system (or status quo) at risk for change with each interaction with others.	Authority is fluid & shared, & is not located in any particular person or job. Rather authority comes from the combination of the situation & the people in the situation. A new situation (or different players) may shift where authority is located. Authority ultimately can support the health of the community & the individual.	Community Supports (Citizen Directed & Controlled)	Resource Partner-Citizen

Consider this a lifelong developmental process, starting from what we know as bureaucratic leadership (oriented to command and control), but striving to evolve our capacities to function as a Change Master or Generative Leader as we pursue citizenship outcomes.

Personal Leadership Development

I started my employment as a personal adjustment counselor with R-Arc after I earned a degree in rehabilitation counseling. My counseling background and skills oriented me to a more supportive leadership approach throughout my career. My first formal position of authority at R-Arc was as the Director of Vocational Services. I believed that functioning as a leader in a legacy setting would entail becoming an expert in one's area of specialization. For me, that was Vocational Rehabilitation. As a Bureaucratic Leader, my expertise was narrow, based on scientific evidence or a prescribed authority documented in a job description and applied within a band of rules and regulations. I employed a command and control style to carry out my duties. The various specializations that were part of our agency were coordinated through a hierarchy of formally anointed general managers. While operating as an expert, I rarely wandered from my world view and I primarily engaged with others in a top-down fashion (although benevolently). This was much the way I functioned as a workshop director – by tempering authoritarian relationships with my counseling background. Bureaucratic leadership aligns with how most of the world defines leadership. It is great for routine, but not for complicated work.

When I was promoted to Associate Executive Director of R-Arc, I began to see the agency operations from a wider vantage point. From this view, other perspectives embedded in the subcultures of Residential and Children Services appeared and I became aware of my own frame of reference. I started to more intentionally act in service to my core values and principles, becoming proficient with management tools such as strategic planning and Total Quality Management. Along with agency administrators, I set standards and managed against them, intervening and adjusting when variances were discovered. Part of a team that was obsessed with satisfying our "customers," we often stated: "let us know what we can do for you," which became our unspoken operating motto. My leadership orientation was as a Technical Leader. Those were the days when problems and solutions were relatively clear and definable, and with the proper technical skills we could figure this stuff out. We often reassured the Board of Directors that "everything was running smoothly."

As we became ethically and practically attracted to an individualized supports orientation, all bets were off. No longer were things clearly defined and knowable. Solutions were not obvious, the work called for partnership, and learning new ways of supporting people replaced "treatment pathways" and programs. Called on to be a Change Master, I found myself facilitating multiple initiatives, working with resistance, as well as creating and overseeing learning infrastructure. This required taking on a variety of perspectives while remaining centered in my own values and beliefs.

I found authority in my personal beliefs, seeing the power of mutual relationships in service of developing individualized supports. Person-centered processes found their way into our organizational practices supported by Change Masters at every level.

Recently, I am tuning into an image of myself facilitating the emergence of healthy and diverse communities who are integrating a variety of perspectives into a wonderfully expressive whole. As such I am working at expanding my capacity as Generative Leader, one who is proficient at creating blue space for social innovation.

Going to Places of Potential

When struggling with solutions to different issues, going to places that offered new perspectives has helped to stop me from automatically (and mindlessly) acting upon my beliefs about people. As I engaged in intensive study, reading books on innovation and leadership, traveling to places of potential and joining with others in a community of practice, I discovered new perspectives and new leadership strategies. Methods such as Communities of Practice and Appreciative Inquiry[45] were particularly effective in developing aspects of my leadership style that align with evolving Integrative and Community Support practices. At R-Arc we used these methods to invite people who shared an interest (e.g., developing oneself as an instrument of change) to learn and develop new capacities. As these are voluntary and organic learning practices, each person must be personally committed to a collective learning process as it unfolds in a series of "U" experiences.

A dialogic process in groups and organizations entail conversations that help us to make sense of our world and a given social context. We learned that skillful dialogue between people is integral to socially innovating supports. By participating in these practices over the years I have discovered that my authentic leadership voice comes from within me rather than from my organizational role. Authentic leadership can be accessed through our multiple intelligences with integrating the intellectual (mind), emotional (heart), spiritual (will), and applied (hand). Operating in concert, and uniquely expressed by each person, these intelligences produce a leadership voice that allows one to function as a Change Master or Generative Leader.

Generative Leadership Practices

Leaders operating from a generative orientation commit to building a healthy whole community, working beyond our self-interest to engage in relationships that reach from personal to global. Practicing generative leadership involves developing a skillset beyond the more traditional forms of organization development, one which focuses on transitioning the system, organization, and team from one defined state to another. This often requires a process of unfreezing, moving, then refreezing the cultural form.

Transformational change demands additional skill sets to work with emerging futures and forms, and to innovate and develop new social relationships. It is an orientation that fosters continual learning and creating solutions to new challenges versus technically solving everyday problems. A Generative Leader can master both orientations, solving problems while creating blue space for innovative practice to emerge. A Generative Leader can simultaneously play by the rules and with the rules as a way to keep the game going. They alternate action with reflecting upon the meaning of their experiences breaking out of rational management processes typically limited to discovering variances to standards and implementing corrections. Generative Leaders engage in multiple loops of learning, and challenge what is normally taken for granted in everyday practice. Their process embodies the disruptive innovative cycle of Theory U.

The different leadership orientations mirror the values, purpose and culture of the stages of the DD system. Each model of support expresses a sensibility that demands certain actions and functions from leaders. These sensibilities emanate from a worldview that births a support model and creates coercive expectations for leadership to take a certain form. The Institutional form and culture perceives the leader as the manifestation of a legally defined role operating within a set of articulated policies and procedures. Within managed care, there is an increased demand to integrate clinical disciplines and manage costs, therefore the Technical Leader is called on to problem solve across varying forms of expertise. When a transformation from care models to support models is needed, a leader is called upon to become a Change Master. The vision of a diverse and socially innovative community requires a leadership that understands the complexities of emergent and unknown futures. The progression from Bureaucrat to Generative Leader is both internally developed by the individual and externally coaxed by organizational context and form. Generative Leaders are not attached to ego-needs as they are community-centric and deeply compassionate. There is directionality to human development and evolving forms of organization from simple to complex, with leadership taking shape in more sophisticated ways to compliment the tasks at hand that transcend and include all support models.

There are examples of people who have skipped developmental stages and functioned in advanced leadership states (e.g. generative leaders in institutional settings). These are people who are ahead of their time, coming up with new ideas and trying new practices. Often, they are considered by many as mavericks, or just plain crazy, though they might be on the leading edge of an emerging support model. In the most regrettable scenarios, they can end up broken or forgotten by an unforgiving system as they were pioneers in bringing forth a new, hopefully better world.

Master practitioners of innovation embrace the notion of "self as an instrument of change." For many of us in the DD field, this often entails shifting our perspectives about people with disabilities, what kind of outcomes are possible, how to provide support in meaningful ways and the kind of roles we assume as service providers. At the center of becoming a virtual instrument of change is the archetypical hero's journey echoed in the developmental process that takes one from Bureaucratic Leader to Generative Leader.[46]

The Trials of the Journey

Traveling on our intentional change journey with my peers at R-Arc, I was faced with many trials. Many were related to external factors such as supports design questions, human resource issues, funding limitations, unfriendly audit environments, and our organization's culture and current practices. Operating in the spirit of an instrument of change I also confronted questions and challenges that surfaced internally, in particular questions related to my assumptions about the capacities of people with disabilities and my confidence in managing change, risk taking and conflict. I have chosen the journey to become a Generative Leader to create space for emerging futures while honoring our organization's legacy and regulatory obligations. This means I aspire to rise above the emotional fray, avoid reactivity and automatic responses, and resist the coercive push of the herd by engaging in deep change practices rather than trying to find quick fixes.

Innovation is both disturbing and exhilarating and can personally challenge the most prepared and emotionally developed, so personal leadership development is critical. The levels of leadership – Bureaucratic, Technician, Change Master and Generative Leader– outlines a developmental understanding of leadership. The levels are not evaluative; instead they describe the emerging stages of deeper understanding and seeing the complexities of our world. Each level is aligned with a DD support model and organizational form, if the support model is functioning well and has utility. As leaders grow towards a generative perspective, they not only see a broader expanse of possibility and diversity, but also sense their connectedness to the universe. These qualities are necessary to bring forth the transformational forms of Integrated and Community Supports.

Becoming an instrument of change challenges leaders to move from a bureaucratic level of competence toward change mastery and ultimately to generative leadership. In this process you need to become a reflective practitioner. A learning log is a tool that aids in gaining awareness of pieces or aspects of oneself that may be hidden, below the level of awareness or unacknowledged brought out through the process of reflective writing. As with larger systems, like our own organizations, when engaging in transformational change, awareness is a key first step in the journey.

Key Points

- Engaging in transforming legacy services to individualized supports requires the presence of generative leadership. These are leaders who develop themselves as instruments of change.

- Effective leaders who are part of transformational change initiatives often describe their experiences in ways that are typical to Joseph Campbell's Hero's Journey.

- Four leadership orientations (Bureaucratic, Technical, Change Master and Generative Leaders) parallel the evolution of DD service models in worldview, relationship, and interaction.

Guided Self or Team Learning Journey

1. Using the Hero's Journey graphic on page 86, identify (prospectively if you or your agency has not started a process to individualize supports) a) what called you to engage in a change journey to individualized supports; b) what routines were disrupted (personally and organizationally); c) what new (support, relational) territories did you travel to?; d) what new perspectives did you have about: people with DD, services and supports, support roles and relationships; e) what new visions did you have for people with DD, your agency, and the supports provided; f) what innovative support practices has your agency prototyped?; and g) what have you and your agency integrated into practice from your learning journey?Complete *Exercise 7: Awakening to Your Calling* (page 168). Share your answers with a peer or in your learning group. Add your responses to your learning journal.

2. Complete *Exercise 8: Finding Your Voice: Becoming the Change You Seek* (page 172). Share your "voice chart" with a peer or your learning group.

3. Review *Becoming a Generative Leader – Self as an Instrument of Change* (page 92). Locate the leadership orientation you most typically exhibit. Share this with a peer or your learning group. Identify the leadership orientation you must assume to facilitate supports transformation. Discuss with others strategies to develop your capacity to assume a more evolved leadership orientation.

8

Shifting Roles and Relationships
Moving Out of Delegation Into Partnership

The most effective way to achieve right relations with any living thing is to look for the best in it, and then help that best into the fullest expression.[47]
—*Allen J. Boone*

If we have learned anything as we evolve our practices, it is that a strong relationship is at the center of individualizing supports. A good relational form with families and individuals is brought forth and nurtured by compassion, appreciative inquiry, and empathic listening rather than clinical technique or diagnostic methodology. As relationships deepen among individuals, families and R-Arc staff, options for self-directed lives and a flexible support role grow, and pathways out of the gridlock of competing commitments become more evident.

Relationships are the nature and form of the connections between people. Roles are defined tasks, assigned responsibilities, and delineated authority to carry out particular functions. Think about a parent's role in a child's nurturance, and how the responsibility shifts to the child as the parent grows elderly. In this relationship, responsibility manifests organically, rooted in love. Compare this with what responsibility connotes for a superintendent who is accountable for the students within their school district. Bureaucracy is impersonal: driven by regulations not reciprocity, professional obligation not humanity.

Bureaucratic forces affect everyone to a certain degree, though most people can rely on their intimate life (relationships, hobbies, spirituality, etc.) to provide a buffer. Imagine that the role of the parent is omitted, and replaced by personnel operating under the superintendent's direction. Providers assume full responsibility to meet all of a person's needs according to terms agreed upon by the person or their legal guardian within the limits set by the funding agencies. In twenty-four hour settings where service provision is most intensive, providers are the primary authority over every aspect of a person's life—in this arrangement, the scope of intimacy is determined by default rather than choice, or else is nonexistent. Moving to Integrative Supports shifts this pattern fundamentally. Roles are negotiated and emergent rather than predefined and assumed by hierarchical structures, and people and their support circles choose to enter a partnership based on trust and shared responsibility rather than delegating the design and delivery of services to providers.

In this chapter the roles and relationships in Institutional and Managed Care Models are contrasted with those found in Integrated Supports. I also look at the capacities we must develop to engage in right relationships with individuals and families to co-design and co-implement individualized supports.

Powerful Shifts in the Form of Our Relationships

We have grown in capacity to form reciprocal and trusting relationships. Some of the most powerful shifts in relational form have emerged when people supported by R-Arc are at the end of their lives. A person with a developmental disability living in a community residence on feeding tubes and a respirator with only months would have been sent to a skilled-nursing facility a short fifteen years ago. Without friends and family to visit, the inevitability of living out the last part of life alone and without joy was taken as "just the way it is." That condition endured until those who cared about Henry took the challenge of creating another way.

> *Henry was supported by R-Arc in an apartment in generic-senior housing. When Henry's illness reached the point where a nursing home referral was typical, R-Arc remained committed to supporting him at home. After some initial fear that they would be unable to do what Henry needed, staff faced his situation with renewed commitment. With some training and nursing oversight, they successfully supported Henry in his new life phase. Staff not only addressed Henry's ongoing medical needs, but got to know him at a deeper level and responded to his interests and desires. Henry enjoyed the ocean, so they obtained a wide screen TV to play ocean scenes and sounds. Henry loved Christmas, so they held a "Christmas in July" celebration (given that it was likely he would not make it to the next December.) It was obvious Henry was experiencing happiness in his last days. Authentic personal connections helped Henry end his journey in a place of joy and comfort. Profoundly moved by the experience, some of Henry's support staff said it was a turning point in their own lives.*

Increasing Our Relational Capacities

Henry's experience reminds me that reciprocity and caring form the core of an evolved support relationship. These evolved, more trusting relationships emerge more from practicing compassion and assuming an appreciative frame of reference than from building communication skills or implementing technologies. From this ethical perspective, our focus shifts from exclusive self-interest to encompass the concerns of another person, as they experience them. It is further deepened when emotional and spiritual intelligence informs our thinking and action. These relationships have qualities of deep knowing and understanding. They reveal something about ourselves and offer us a path to deeper insight into the meaning of our world. This sensibility, when applied in our workplace, triggers us to intentionally create caring communities that honor difference, share power positively, and foster holistic well-being.

From Power Over to Power With

How power and influence are exercised is a critical factor in building trusting partnerships with individuals and families. As a more mature and mutual relationship develops, the shift from "power over" to "power with" occurs. This distinction, noted by social worker and management theorist Mary Parker Follett in 1924, describes the power over dynamics seen in institutional and managed care environments. The power holder actively directs or influences the passive receiver, as in a doctor diagnosing a malady and prescribing treatment, because the expert is assumed to think and speak the truth. This is the prototypical expert-patient relationship. This kind of power arrangement lingers in our legacy services and in many of the rules applied in our system. For individuals to be supported in person-centered ways and ultimately as citizens, a relational shift that enacts "power with" must occur. Carl Rogers' person-centered approach to understanding human relations in therapeutic situations[48] and person-centered planning with individuals with developmental disabilities underscore the humanistic imperative to embrace "power with". A "power with" dynamic positions interacting parties in a reciprocal process of mutual and satisfying social exchanges. This is a dialogue with each participating party seeing themselves as an interdependent part of something larger. At its most evolved state, the conversation is a vehicle to enact new social arrangements. It is a positive form of power that encourages relational well-being and the health of a collective community. In an organizational form, collaboration becomes the primary mode of operation with a triple bottom line of people, planet, and profit (or for non-profits, mission).

Appreciating Difference

A power with dynamic requires that we recognize the best in people and must truly care about and appreciate others in their everyday world. Our caring stems from the belief that we are all connected therefore our individual fates are uniquely intertwined. This is not assuming the one-up position of paternalistic caring, but pursuing a determined interest in finding sustainable solutions for everyone. Just as the pond supports a diverse web of life, healthy communities link all of us together. As we open ourselves to more ways of knowing we can respectfully and productively engage a greater range of differences in values, abilities, and capacities for expression.

Control Mind-Set

The extent to which we can actualize person-centered supports depends on our mindset. Most agencies and their employees operating within the Institutional and Managed Care Models enact their roles through command and control because they have been designated in charge of the person. This mindset blindly assumes that staff know what is best for the people they serve and are responsible for controlling their behaviors. Families and individuals who accept the delegated support arrangement explicit in the Institutional and Managed Care Models usually share this perspective, or at least leave it unquestioned.

Most institutional settings operate on the assumption that relationships will be detached, instrumental, and impersonal and that clearly prescribed and well-monitored roles are the best ways to avoid neglect or abuse. The human spirit may transcend these structures and enact warm and caring connections but the official story of the organization is one of well-policed role boundaries with those in authority responsible for systems of bureaucratic control.

When operating from within the control mindset, providers perceive that they understand the situation and are right and pure, so their feelings and actions are justified. If families and individuals disagree with the provider, they are wrong, don't understand, and have questionable motives. To further aggravate this, providers keep much of their thinking private while at the same time strongly advocating for their position and ignoring family or individual points of view. Mostly, the provider professionally manipulates the process and covers up all their subtle maneuvers with declarations of person-centeredness. In addition, some professional ethical standards promote a detached stance to maintain professional distance. Instead of openly working through these unproductive power dynamics providers engage in a defensive dance. Without restructuring one's mind-set from control to mutual learning, people stay stuck in the Institutional or Managed Care perspective. [49]

Mutual Learning Mind-Set

A trusting relationship requires a mutual learning mind-set. Here we strongly believe we are interconnected at a universal and community level. We all bring something to the table, whether it is resources, information, or different points of view on a complex situation. Emphasizing respect, curiosity and appreciation we assume one another's integrity within our individual understanding of the possibilities in our shared situation. Ultimately we share what we know in transparent ways, and when in partnership hold each other jointly accountable for outcomes.

To bring a mutual learning mind-set into practice requires a degree of emotional maturity and self-awareness. Emotional intelligence has been defined as self and relational-awareness and the ability to act with intention as informed by this insight. Recently Goleman and others have identified emotional intelligence as a key ingredient of personal effectiveness at work and in life. Increasing our emotional intelligence is prerequisite to enacting enlightened relationships.

Enacting an Enlightened Relationship

As a support provider operating from a commitment to person-centered practice, we must be available to approach our work with individuals and families from an appreciative point of view. This step is necessary before we can make meaningful contact with individuals and families leading to a collaborative relational form. To authentically partner with individuals and families from a co-constructive approach, the provider must suspend judgment (I am right, they are wrong), cynicism (been there, done that), and fear (I feel lost in the new support model or who will I be if not an expert.) In the enlightened relationship we must be willing to witness (as opposed to directing) or collaborate with an individual and family moving from dependency and client-hood to self-direction and citizenship. Instead of monolithic representations of clients, we must be open to the individual's life processes unfolding among us. In this context, good form relates to how we interact with individuals and families.

The Process of Enlightened Relationship

Achieving a trusting and enlightened relationship is primarily realized by having good conversations and time well spent with each other. A successful interaction moves us empathically into the other person's life experience. This takes some energy, so we must be motivated by and committed to the possibility of a mutual exchange. When we cannot sustain our energy, engagement is disrupted and leaves everyone in a condition of "unfinished business." Unsatisfying interactions that accumulate often result in a breakdown between individuals, families, and their providers. It is especially critical in high-interaction support models to pay attention to the energy with which we are listening and conversing: when each party displays mutual appreciation for what the other brings to the table, what is on the table becomes shared.

Unlike managed care processes, which shortcut the development of learning relationships with diagnostic pathways and assessment tools, Integrated and Community Support Models require time and intentionality. Like a low-simmering stew, the enlightened relationship takes some time to cook. No shortcuts, no microwave options, this is old-fashioned "getting to know you". Here it is important to embrace the maxim "go slow to go fast." It is necessary to allow time for relationships to deepen and emergent solutions to percolate. Mutual ownership coupled with complete and satisfying conversations build the necessary trust to engage in co-designing support arrangements.[50]

Deep Listening and Deep Dives

> *In music… you don't make bad notes… the note next to the one you think is 'bad', corrects the one in front."* [51]
>
> —Miles Davis

Not honoring the rhythm and pace of creating new practices creates the conditions for gridlock. Bureaucrats listen for information that fits within a set of policies and procedures. Assisting a person to apply for government benefits fits this listening mode. Bureaucratic process does not require an understanding of other points of view. Program administrators and clinicians must listen for the customer's interest and stated needs in order to develop a satisfying response.

In an enlightened relationship there are no mistakes, only opportunities for learning and growth. We move through levels of listening by discarding the bureaucratic listening structure to better hear the sound of another's worldview. This informs reflection on what our shared purpose and partnership asks of us. Immersing ourselves in enlightened relationships ignites premonition of future lifestyle possibilities in the community outside a service program. The diagram summarizes the evolution of listening.

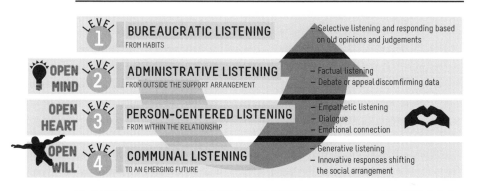

EVOLUTIONARY
Listening and Responding Practices

	LEVEL 1	BUREAUCRATIC LISTENING	– Selective listening and responding based
		FROM HABITS	on old opinions and judgements
OPEN MIND	LEVEL 2	ADMINISTRATIVE LISTENING	– Factual listening
		FROM OUTSIDE THE SUPPORT ARRANGEMENT	– Debate or appeal discomfirming data
OPEN HEART	LEVEL 3	PERSON-CENTERED LISTENING	– Empathetic listening
		FROM WITHIN THE RELATIONSHIP	– Dialogue
			– Emotional connection
OPEN WILL	LEVEL 4	COMMUNAL LISTENING	– Generative listening
		TO AN EMERGING FUTURE	– Innovative responses shifting
			the social arrangement

Inspired by Otto Scharmer

One of the best examples we have of a trusting and mutual relationship with a parent is with Connell Frazer.

> *Our journey with Connell and her sons consisted of trials and challenges that shifted our perceptions and our support practices over the years. I met Connell over twenty years ago in her role as the Dean of Special Education in a local college. I had reached out to her as a resource for an international project I was working on with the Partners of the Americas program. Connell had come my way through a recommendation that raved about her skills and progressive views about inclusion of people with disabilities. Early on in the project, I discovered that Connell had adopted two boys with severe disabilities, and many years later adopted a young girl. I was impressed then, as I am now, with her commitment to her children, but what struck me even more was her relentless advocacy around seeking a "normal" life for both of her boys.*
>
> *Years later Connell approached R-Arc with a request to support Jim, her oldest son, and then a few years later with another request to support David. This initiated a journey of discovery, in finding and supporting Jim's and David's interests and capacities, but also for our organization. R-Arc continually designed and redesigned supports, negotiated roles and relation-*

ships with Connell, and pushed the envelope around the highest possible degree of self-direction and autonomy for her sons. I can't even begin to count the number of times support arrangements were undone and reconstructed with the hands-on support alternating between Connell and R-Arc staff. For example, the first year after graduating from high school, Jim moved into his own apartment with R-Arc staff support. After a series of near-miss disasters, Jim moved to one of our group homes to live with five other people. This was our best guess at the time in providing enough staff to stabilize Jim's living arrangement, and to keep him safe. At that time no one, Connell, Jim or R-Arc staff, felt this was a move forward for Jim.

Connell saw Jim was disturbing the household for others, and made the decision to move Jim back to her home. A few years later, we developed a three-person living situation which was implemented based on a person-centered plan. Again, this support arrangement was a result of our collective judgment on how to provide enough support for Jim to live "least restrictively" in the community. Jim and the two other gentlemen then moved to another location.

The next change involved the two other men moving out leaving Jim to live a single life with 24/7 staff support. Through all these experiences, Jim exhibited aggressive behavior towards others, and was often self-abusive. Experts of every ilk spun theories, made educated guesses and overall "winged it" in terms of diagnosing Jim's "issues." Medications were prescribed, tracked, altered and dropped, with no luck in getting Jim to settle down. Connell recalled at one time that her family had been "person-centered planned," "essential life-styled" and "ISPed" ad nauseam. Given that Jim tended to "mellow out" when they traveled down to Georgia to visit with her parents, Connell hypothesized that Jim might do better living with her for a while. Connell suggested that she and her daughter move into the now former certified residence to live with Jim. The assumption was that Connell's relationship was a key ingredient in grounding Jim, and the revolving nature of shift staff caused him to obsess and get anxious waiting for people to show up.

Obviously, this was highly unusual and possibly never before attempted in a "certified site" in New York State. This arrangement needed all sorts of pretzel-like machinations on the part of our agency and the state system: not least the question of how to apply regulations designed for provider controlled housing in a newly invented family/provider collaborative. Ultimately, a highly organic mixture of flexible R-Arc staffing support, R-Arc owned housing, Medicaid funding and Connell's support presence has had a significant impact on Jim's life. Jim's behavioral events have been reduced to close to zero, and he enjoys working and hanging out in Troy. Proving the level of commitment it takes to help shape a meaningful life experience, this story is only a small slice of the journey with Connell and her sons.

The experiences we have with Connell and her sons conjure up a vision of a future in which co-designed support arrangements are the norm. The thinking and the actions of Connell and R-Arc exemplify an evolutionary relationship indicative of the Integrated Supports Model. None of this would have been possible without deepening our listening practices. Our everyday collaboration with Connell and her sons provides a glimpse into the potential of innovation resulting from a shift in belief, practice, and relationship.

One might hope to find a prescription instructing providers how to move directly into partnerships with individuals and families. However, our experience with Connell and her sons indicates that this is a wasteful search. Admitting that true person-centered approaches inherently oppose the traditional models doesn't free us from our obligations to legacy services. It does at least allow us to move past the expert-patient paradigm and orients us to an infinite future of inquisition and innovation.

Modes of Creating a Support Plan

Roles that we might share with individuals and families become clearer when we are open to examining the different ways a support plan is created. The following chart lays out the various ways that service providers, individuals, and families can create an individual service or support plan. Within the Institutional and Managed Care Models, services are dictated or advertised to individual "clients" or "consumers." Key programmatic decisions are made by the providers and communicated to service recipients. The level of engagement and commitment is low and revolves around compliance. As services transform into supports in Integrated and Community Supports Models, the plans, strategies, and support arrangements are negotiated or co-created. Decisions are now shared by all or self-directed by individuals and families. Communications are horizontal and mutual. As supports are co-created, engagement and commitment to process and outcomes are high.

Five Modes of Creating a Support Plan

	Tell (Demand Compliance)	Sell (Seek Buy-In)	Test (Invite Response)	Consult (Request Input)	Co-Create (Collaborate)
Does the plan or program already exist?	Yes, final form	Yes, final form	Draft form	No	No
Who decides on the final plan, program, or supports?	Provider, state agency	Managed Care organization	Managed Care organization and individual and family	Individual, family and provider	Individual and family with provider

Communica-tion Method	Top down transmission of informa-tion	Top down transmission of informa-tion	Top down and bottom up transmission of information	Negotia-tion and Dialogue	Deep dives and dialogue
Level of Engagement & Commitment	Low	Low	Medium	High	High
Care or Support Model	Institutional Care	Managed Care	Managed Care	Integrated Supports	Community Supports

A few years ago, the typical R-Arc "intake" process entailed either telling a potential "consumer" what is available or selling them on a particular intervention. Intake, as we know it in Institutional and Managed Care Service Models, requires families and individuals to be paraded in front of a care coordination team. After introductions, the meeting reviews the potential openings, spaces or available bed, for which the person may qualify. The meeting proceeds with a revealing presentation of the individual's profile replete with intimate details about their needs and deficits. The family and individual feel exposed and intimidated in the company of strangers, and are often relegated to passive roles, answering questions only if asked. Having no say as to whether they are "accepted into program," they are experiencing a power over process.

> *Conversely, our staff was invited into the living room of Abby's parent's home, to plan for and design a living arrangement for their daughter. Sandy, our Director of Innovation, explored the interests, desires, and needs of Abby and her parents to determine a supportive pathway for Abby's next life stage to unfold. Ahead of the curve, and ready for this exciting next step, Abby had already identified a person to live with her. Abby's parents said they wanted her apartment close to the family home so they could stay in close contact with her. Respecting this request, Sandy negotiated the details of the support arrangement with Abby's parents, a particularly critical conversation given that they wanted to stay involved and present in her life. They were specifically interested in coordinating all her medical appointments. Agreeing to follow any regulatory guidelines that the State of New York had in this area, Abby's parents felt comfortable with supports including a paid neighbor, who would live in an apartment next to Abby and her roommate. The paid neighbor would be provided a free apartment in exchange for their availability to respond to emergencies or spend social time with Abby, entailing about ten hours of committed time a week. Additionally, Abby and her roommate worked with paid R-Arc staff for a designated*

period during the day. This arrangement, customized to every person's needs in the family, allowed for needed supervision, mentorship, and safety, while providing for the maximum amount of personal autonomy for Abby. This arrangement worked for a while until it became apparent Abby and her roommate were incompatible. We are now in the process of finding Abby her own place. It is critical to be flexible in supporting a person's life process rather than simply finding them a placement.

These contrasting processes of offering support vividly illustrate the shift from a care model to a support model. In the first example, an individual and family cross the threshold of the agency and are evaluated as to their suitability for standard services. In Abby's situation, R-Arc's staff crossed the threshold of the family's home to join with Abby and her parent's to figure out the next steps in her life journey.

Evolving Roles of Individuals, Families and Providers

As R-Arc journey unfolds, we continually ask two basic questions: what is the optimal form of our relationship with individuals and families, and what roles do we play in this good relational form? At various points in our evolutionary process different answers to these questions surfaced. I suspect none of them were wrong, as they are part of a developmental process experienced by each one of us, our agencies, and the larger environmental context of the developmental disability field. No judgment is intended as we reflect on the nature of the evolving "professional-individual-caregiver" roles and relationships. Our roles originate from our perceptions of people with DD and what they need. The diagram on the next page illustrates our shifting views and resulting role changes as the system reaches for the support models. As a system evolves to transcend and include developing practices, the roles of providers must also mature while keeping the range of roles available as needed.[52]

Institutional Roles

Early in the history of R-Arc artifacts from the institutional system remained in our services and provider roles. Highly prescriptive processes and often – mechanistic outcomes (slots and beds) structured the service experiences of individuals and families. Like other providers, we had experts: social workers, rehabilitation counselors, psychologists, and a myriad of therapists who figured out the needs of individuals and prescribed treatment. Individuals and families were patients to be cured and passive recipients of direction, advice, treatment, and placements. This is a delegated system of care, where there is an intentional distance between "providers of care" and "users or recipients of care," with higher status and power attached to the providers. An unintended, yet common, outcome of the delegated service system is that the recipient becomes more dependent rather than more resourceful. This bypass of the abundant and priceless resources of people and their families is an unfortunate waste.

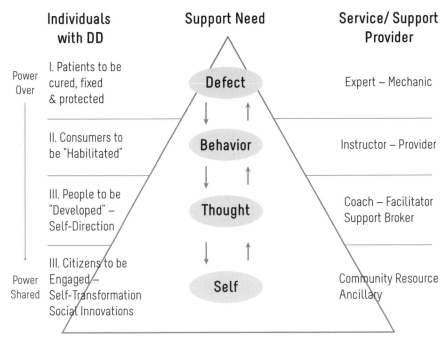

Individuals with DD	Support Need	Service/ Support Provider

| Power Over | I. Patients to be cured, fixed & protected | Defect | Expert – Mechanic |

| | II. Consumers to be "Habilitated" | Behavior | Instructor – Provider |

| | III. People to be "Developed" – Self-Direction | Thought | Coach – Facilitator Support Broker |

| Power Shared | III. Citizens to be Engaged – Self-Transformation Social Innovations | Self | Community Resource Ancillary |

**LEVELS OF INDIVIDUAL–SUPPORT PROVIDER
RELATIONSHIP**

The Transition to Managed Care Roles

Programs conceptualized and designed at the systems level within the Institutional Model were quickly codified by regulations and rolled out across the state. This first wave of the Managed Care Model offered what some saw as localized mini-institutions. As such, the first Managed Care programs retained much of the sensibility of the Institutional Model. As a program type failed to meet people's needs, a solution was derived by defining the particular deficiencies of the identified group (e.g., people with behavior problems), and then implementing a revised program type specialized to those deficiencies. In this situation, individuals with developmental disabilities were perceived as only a step away from being patients to be cured, fixed, or protected. New terminology referred to individuals as clients, yet the individual-provider relationship shifted only slightly. Like most service providers, R-ARC remained in a largely beneficent expert (mechanic) role, retaining the institutional power over status as the service responsibility moved from large institutions to community-based programs. Input of individuals and families into decision-making remained constricted to few options within a largely prescribed service environment. Options offered, such as a "bed" in a community residence, were either accepted or not, with no opportunity to negotiate the features of a support arrangement. We wondered why individuals and families were resistant and we even attended workshops on how to deal with the resistant client or the difficult family.

New Managed Care Roles

The Home and Community Based Waiver (HCBS) brought increased funding and deepened the move into the Managed Care Model by awakening the provider community and federal/state policy functionaries to the limitations of the lingering Institutional Model. As the number of "clients" began stacking up in programs, placements started looking more like holding tanks and developmental dead-ends than bridges to community living. Individuals ended up running in place rather than moving along the continuum of services. I clearly remember a light bulb going off in my head as I walked past John sitting in the same seat in the work center as he had years before when I worked there as a personal adjustment training counselor. My assumption about the efficacy of our services was severely challenged at that moment: so much for building work readiness for competitive placements. It was then that I joined with my fellow evolutionary travelers to find alternative ways to support people.

We saw the HCBS waiver as a solution to the stuckness of group-based programming and a way to move people along service pathways to community presence and participation. The step away from programs to face-to-face services redefined clients as consumers to be habilitated. Now providers shifted their exclusive focus from managing deficiencies to assisting consumers to develop behavioral capacities. New roles emerged focused on instruction and offering services specified by an "individual service plan" that will prepare and connect individuals to community settings.

The most recent iteration of Managed Care focuses on reducing cost. This is done through administrative structures that integrate acute health care and long-term care under a single management entity. The primary function of this entity is the provision of care coordination to assist individuals in navigating complex health care systems to avoid duplication and unnecessary services and prevent more costly health conditions from occurring. A power over role orientation continues in the process of "managing care:" the image of care manager does not suggest an equal collaborator. The label "consumer" was intended to re-position the individual and family as the purchaser of services. The unfulfilled premise is that consumers have a marketplace of service and provider alternatives from which to choose, and because this marketplace has yet to develop, the power of the consumer to purchase services or walk elsewhere with their money is little more than a hollow promise. Roles and relationships between people and their providers remain largely hierarchical and delegated in nature within managed care.

Mutual and Self-Directed Roles

Moving from a public relations sound bite, person-centered planning jumps off the agency brochure and moves into everyday practice. By dislodging supports from a programmatic structure, integrated supports frees up resources to be organized around a person. Here is where people with disabilities begin to experience what many of us already have. They are valued for their respective gifts and are welcomed to take on contributing roles in the community. As such, the provider-function transforms from caretaker or habilitation instructor into coach, facilitator, and support broker to help assemble the resources necessary to get such outcomes as a job, a home of one's own, and relationships that express intimacy for an individual who is self-directing their life. The Integrated Supports Model is where the espoused values begin to catch up with provider actions leading to valued outcomes for people.

On the Supports Horizon

On our supports horizon is the citizen-centered Community Supports Model. Our work with Connell and her sons is centered in the Integrative Support Model, but position us to view the Community Supports Model in the distance. This is the creative edge of our work in which individuals and their families and their chosen partners are engaged in planning, designing, and implementing their supports. The idea here is that individuals can develop solutions for themselves in partnership with an evolving service provider, rather than delegating this task to a service system as the community becomes a place of acceptance and resource. This is not meant to operate as a cover for a governmental retreat from responsibility to support disadvantaged populations. It is about a substantial realignment of relationships – from those functioning in delegated care arrangement to those that promote self-responsibility and individual contribution within a society that cares about the collective health of its communities.

Examples of the Community Supports Model appear when the individual can directly purchase or get the personal assistance they need from a provider to function as an autonomous citizen in their community. Some of the creative support arrangements that R-Arc currently offers take the form of paid-neighbors and live-in or next-to personal assistance paid for by government funds. These forms of support reduce the level of service provider intrusiveness and allow for a maximum amount of personal freedom for the individual. Creating Community Supports forms often afford an opportunity to build, extend or enhance community in a world currently dominated by monolithic service systems. It has been the experience of ours that when we intentionally come together with families, individuals, and their friends to design this type of support arrangement, we are evoking this vision of a more diverse and inclusive community in the process.

A realignment of support relationships becomes a possibility within a newly created arrangement, one that is not reflected in the market economy or exclusively a result of distributing resources through the government and its service providing agents. Innovation, as we typically think of it, happens in the private for-profit sector. But the emergence of a more inclusive community calls for social innovation, the co-creation of personalized solutions in vibrant blue spaces that encourage co-creation between government agencies, the civil sector, the business community, the non-profit providers, and individual citizens in their households. Blue space is the place of potential, given that no one sector "owns the problem," but all sectors voluntarily join in the struggle to bring forth new strategies to address complex, stuck problems. Social innovation derives from mutual exchange and collaborative effort. This supports orientation is perhaps the only one that can claim true transformation of client-hood to citizenship for people with developmental disabilities. Within the Community Supports Model engaged networks co-design and co-implement supports.

We have learned that certain key elements consistently appear when services are successfully co-created with individuals and families. The boundaries between sectors (e.g., public, private, household) are redrawn, and the work of designing and implementing becomes less formally arranged and more organic in quality. The following table summarizes these functioning elements in co-designed supports – how many do you see operating in your agency?

Co-Created Supports

Recognizing people as assets	Shifting mental models from passive recipients of services and burdens on the system to equal partners with providers.
Building on an individual's existing capacities	Shifting mental models (embedded perceptions) of individuals with disabilities from being deficient to being capable.
Mutuality and reciprocity	Engage individuals and providers in reciprocal and right relationships.
Personal and Peer Networks	Connect and nurture networks among stakeholders and providers (e.g., communities of practice).
Sharing Roles and Tasks	Sharing the roles and tasks between all holders by co-creating (designing and implementing) services and supports.
Facilitating rather than delivering	Provider assuming change catalyst and facilitator functions rather than central providers of service.

Chapter 9 turns to the actual look and feel of individualized supports in their low and high applications.

Key Points

- Trusting and mutual relationships between individuals, families, and providers are foundational to effectively designing and implementing individualized supports.

- Key to enlightened provider-individual relationships is shifting from power over to power with social arrangements.

- Enlightened relationships are developed through deep listening and responding practices. This process entails listening beyond our preconceptions and just the facts to connecting with the felt experience of another and what the larger community is asking of us.

- Roles of individuals, families, and providers change in the movement from care to support models. The roles increase in variety, type, and application as other support models transcend and include previous models of care. These roles touch on creating plans to providing supports with and to individuals with DD.

Guided Self or Team Learning Journey

1. How would you describe the relationships the members of your agency have with families and individuals? Are they professional and hierarchical or are they mutual and partnership-oriented? Is power shared or attributed to one group or another?

2. Review *Evolutionary Listening and Responding Practices* (page 104).Which listening practices do you apply and feel most comfortable with in your job or role? What levels of listening do you need to experience and develop?

3. Review *Five Modes of Creating a Support Plan* (page 106). Which mode is most frequently used in your agency? Assess the impact of this mode on the communication and relationships you have with individuals and families? What outcomes or results are achieved for the individuals served by your agency? Can you imagine trying another mode of creating a plan and what impact would this have on developing individualized supports?

4. Perform *Exercise 9: Individual/Provider Roles.* (page 173). Looking at the on provider-individual roles (page 109), what are the roles assumed by members and individuals in your agency's services? Consider the differences between someone who is a client, a consumer and a citizen. Which of these roles does your agency promote?

5. In reviewing *Key Elements of Co-Created Supports* (page 112), how many are present in your agency and to what degree? Can you give concrete examples of these elements in the daily life of your organization?

Abby Phillips story is told in Chapter 8

9

Individualizing Supports
Many Degrees of Application

To be yourself in a world that is constantly trying to make you something else is the greatest accomplishment. [53]

—*Ralph Waldo Emerson*

Our direction of travel is clear: we want to move away from the group based Institutional Care Model to Community Supports, where we respond to each individual's uniqueness rather than downloading programs and practices based on a particular diagnosis.

A key theme in our journey has been in developing an understanding of the many shapes and forms of individualization. This has helped us get unstuck from our competing commitments as a legacy service provider by unlocking an either/or dynamic.

A Definition of Individualized Support

This is how a group of self-advocates, parent advocates and providers convened by the Self-Advocacy Association of New York State understands individualized supports:[54]

> We define individualized supports as an array of supports, services and resources that are person-centered, based on the unique interests and needs of the person, afford the person as much control over their supports as they desire, and are adaptable as the person's life changes. This means that supports are created around an individual's distinct vision for their life rather than created around a facility or funding stream.

The Pitfalls of Co-Opting Terminology

It is easier to espouse one's values than to enact them. An agency may state on its web site that it engages in person-centered planning and offers individualized supports, while in practice it carries out routine admissions processes that place those accepted into program "slots" or "beds." Individualizing supports is seen as the fad of the day: the often unrecognized dissonance between what we say we value and how our organization behaves gets our practice stuck, reinforces an experience of incompetence, sends confusing messages, and results in widespread cynicism. Cynicism dissolves as the practice honors the intent of the espoused value and its ethical essence. The first step is acknowledging this gap and accepting responsibility to close it.

Another potential misreading of this term relates to the concept of perpetual individualization,[55] which refers to the decline of civic engagement and the undermining of social capital by relentless pursuit of self-interest. Contrary to this notion, individualized supports are not intended to be exclusively self-interest oriented: an equally important part of the mission is to open up possibilities of valued civic roles and contribution.

Our Supports Become More Individualized As R-Arc's Intentional Journey Unfolds

As our service models evolve, both our understanding and our practice of individualized supports change their shape. Around the time when I joined the R-Arc as a Personal Adjustment Training Counselor in 1979, an individualized support, at that time, was reflected in the process of teaching individuals how to perform production assembly work using Marc Gold's, *Try Another Way* technology.[56] A few years later, R-Arc staff claimed that individualized services were part of our continuum of service offerings. Here, an individual theoretically graduated from one service offering to another as they achieved certain competencies by meeting goals set in their individual service plan. We justified this approach as individualized by claiming the appropriateness of a service or placement was determined by the results of an individual needs assessment. Another phase of individualizing services entailed a form of Burger King's "have it your way" service experience. From a menu of limited choices, an individual could select different features of a service (usually in a group-based facility) at different time intervals. For example, an individual might choose between a crafts activity and sorting change as part of a personal skills development program. Almost imperceptively at first, we began to decouple the support from a location – a community residence, day treatment program, or sheltered workshop – by supporting people in their own home and/or a job.

This table describes how the concept of individualized supports assumes different forms within different DD support orientations.

Support Orientation	Institutional Care	Managed Care	Integrated Supports	Community Supports
Manifestations of Individualized Support Through the Evolutionary Stages	Menu of Services in Provider Program Settings	Customized Services in Provider Program Settings	Decoupled Services and Individually Designed Supports Outside Provider Settings	Completely Self-directed or Co-designed Supports in Individual's Own Home

The levels of individualized support can be translated into descriptive examples and arrayed from low to high levels of individualization. The levels' structure can be used to identify the degree to which a legacy provider individualizes supports. With this information, strategies can be developed to incrementally evolve individualized supports to match a provider's capacity and growing awareness of design possibilities.

Elements of Individualized Supports

We believe that physical wellness, positive relationships with friends and family, enacting valued roles in one's community, and a stable and functional home life provide the conditions for a life of distinction for all people. A life of distinction unfolds in a process of self-definition and choices about lifestyle. Those who are self-directing their life experience a significant degree of:

- Choice (have options from which to choose)
- Decision making (have a role in making decisions)
- Control (have control over aspects of their life space and resources)
- Involvement (in the settings where they spend their lives and their community)

As the field of developmental disabilities progresses towards self-determination and a person-first orientation, services (and the system) need to achieve higher levels of individualized supports. Presently, we find people with developmental disabilities in a variety of settings: at home, in legacy programs, or living in their own homes and filling contributing community roles with the assistance they require. While legacy settings are usually more constrained in the choices they can offer, any of these places can offer real opportunities for a vibrant life, stability, and safety, or degenerate into a life of deprivation and impoverishment. The operating assumptions underlying self-determination and individualized supports include:

People with developmental disabilities and their families can develop capacities to engage in self-determination and are accountable and responsible stewards of public funds.

Support providers can work in partnership and co-created social arrangements to modify and support the realization of valued self-directed outcomes with individuals and families.

The way to support self-directed outcomes is by varying the application (or level) of individualized support to match individual need, circumstance, and the context and readiness of a legacy organization.

Level of Individualization

We have found that every setting, including our legacy services, can increase the level of individualization. This happens by identifying where people, program, and practices are now and trying a series of innovations at a risk level that staff, families and individuals can tolerate. Over time, this has resulted in different levels of individualization that enable different degrees of self-direction. R-Arc's efforts at individualization can be described on three levels, which are:

- Low: Working in the box of traditionally structured programs with quality improvement processes and strategies. (Level 1)

- Medium: Re-engineering the box by taking apart some of the traditional programs and reconstructing the supports around the individual. Medium levels of individualization are achieved through redesigning and reinvesting a traditional resource to implement a person-centered plan. (Level 2)

- High: Operating out of the box by avoiding the use of traditional programs and partnering with individuals and families on designing and implementing their budget and set of supports. (Level 3)

This table further defines each level of individualization and the types of supports offered at each level.

How Individualized is the Support?	Types of Individualized Supports	Degree of Choice (range, variety and life options)	Degree of Decision Making (participation and self-direction)	Degree of Personal Space & Ownership (control of resources)	Degree of Social Integration (valued roles)
Low (Focus on Customizing or Modifying Current Practices and Service Environments)	• Person-Centered Planning Leading to Individual Supports in Daily Routines in Program • Expanded Menu of Options Community Outings	• Provides a Menu of Services • Choices Regarding Daily Routines • Choices about activities in which to participate	• Assists Individual in Making Decisions Around Daily Schedule, Meals, Decorating of Common and Personal Space • Input Regarding Program Activities	• Downsizes a Home So Individual has Their Own Bedroom • Provides Opportunity to Select Housemates	• Assists Individual in Experiencing & Being Present in the Community on a Weekly Basis • Participates in a Small Group that Visits or Volunteers in Community Sites

How Individualized is the Support?	Types of Individualized Supports	Degree of Choice (range, variety and life options)	Degree of Decision Making (participation and self-direction)	Degree of Personal Space & Ownership (control of resources)	Degree of Social Integration (valued roles)
Medium (Focus on Designing Individualized Services and Support Environments)	• Person-Centered Designs • Shared Living • Alternative Staffing Arrangements (Live-In, Paid Neighbors) • Supported Employment • Life Coach • Agency with Choice (1)	Assists the Individual/ Family to Assume Primary Decision Making Roles Regarding Hiring Staff, How Quality is Defined, Spending of Personal Allowance Funds, Decorating Living Space	• Provides Choices to the Individual/Family Regarding Living Arrangements (Where/ Whom), Type of Job, Kind of Life Style • Finding a Suitable Location, and Setting Up the Home to the Specifications of the Individual	Supports Individual in Designing a Home Situation	Supports the Individual in Participating in the Community at a Job, Place of Worship, and with as Association on a Frequent or as Desired Basis
High (Focus on Supporting Self-Determination)	• Support uniquely tailored (wraparound) • Support Scenarios (options to select from) • Mix of natural and paid providers. • Support Broker • Fiscal Intermediary • Agency of Choice (2)	Choices Provided to Individual in Key Life Areas (Relationship, Home, Health, Work)	Individual and Family are Supported in Primary Decision Making Roles (Finance and Budget, Vocation, Life Style)	• Assist Individual in Owning or Leasing Own Their Home. • Individual Budget • Cash and Counseling • Home of your own	Supports Individual to Play Active and Primary Roles in Friendship, Marriage, Associational Life, and Employment (outside paid staff arrangements)

High Level: Co-Created Individualization

At its highest levels, individualization should not be confused with customization. When we customize a product, we are tinkering with add-ons to a basic platform, as in options for a car. Customization occurs when an individual selects one or more of a variety of offerings without taking the whole bundle of services a provider offers. This is Level 1 or 2 individualization as defined in the chart above where individuals pick and choose from what is already available. Conversely Level 3 individualization moves beyond customizing supports through interactions between the person and provider involving co-planning, co-designing, and co-implementing supports.

High levels of individualization are constructed from scratch: the respective parties are working "out of the box" of traditionally defined services and roles without a set time limit. The supports are decoupled from a program, constructing an arrangement from the elemental resources.

This organic process includes an identification of a person's needs and life-style interests along with designing creative ways of accommodating the person in natural settings with resources contributed by person, family, community, and provider. Level 3 techniques are used for tailoring the supports to user's personal needs. Tailored supports can be either for the "captured" client interested in being liberated from a segregated setting or an autonomous person residing in the community, who need some specialized personalized supports to holistically function as a citizen.

In Level 3, the numbers of factors to work with are a never-ending emergent reality, made dynamic by ongoing and compounding interactions. Duration of these arrangements may vary from 24/7 supports to partial days to intermittent and variable. Complexity increases with an integrated support arrangement as services can be constructed, deconstructed and rearranged, as opposed to the relative stability of a traditionally structured program. This shifts provider as the controlling authority in service decisions to one voice of influence in a team dynamic.

One example of a high level of individualization was reflected in the process of planning and designing the support arrangements for Bill.

> *Not interested in a program designed for people with developmental disabilities, Bill's support plan was completely co-designed with his family, and facilitated by Sandy. Actively involved in the tapestry of life, Bill spends his time volunteering at a day care center, creating art and ceramics, and developing his skills in Seido Karate. Given his passionate existence, Bill's interest was to live in a downtown location in Troy where he could easily walk to local shops near his own apartment. To respond to Bill's desires and needs, R-Arc provides eight to ten hours of support per day, in addition to the ongoing support of his parents. Bill and his parents express a high degree of satisfaction with their involvement from planning to implementation of this creative arrangement.*

This example of a high degree of individualization is social innovation. Therefore, all participants must be on-board with this way of doing business. It demands creative capacity and emotional maturity from the provider at the individual, team, and/or organization level as well as from the individual and their family. A caution with a "high" support arrangement is that if the service puzzle gets reconstructed with legacy services and its elemental pieces, reactionary state policies or a workforce crisis could push the orientation back to a lower level of individualization.

Low Level: Individualization in Legacy Settings

A lower but important degree of individualization is possible in traditional program settings when standardized services are customized for an individual or group of individuals. This requires an organizational capacity for continuous improvement, customer service, and a technical ability to work creatively "within the box." An example from our agency involved adding community outings, volunteer work, then supported employment a few hours a week to the menu of services offered by our group day habilitation program located in a large facility in Brunswick, N.Y. With people attending our work center, we have added part-time support for individual volunteer opportunities in surrounding neighborhoods. Other examples of Level 1 individualization include adding an art class within the facility. We have discovered that creating art in various media taps a depth of expression that lay hidden for many years in some people.

Medium Level of Individualization: Reinvesting Legacy Resources

Level 2 individualization can be seen as a "tailored" or "redesigned" set of resources that originally were organized in a standardized program format. Service deconstruction and reassembly is commonly provoked by dissatisfaction with a one-size-fits-all service that is unresponsive to individual need. A creative employee in a legacy service with a technical flair for supports redesign may be able to transform traditional services and resources into a uniquely constructed support situation. Many of the same provider capacities required for highly individualized supports apply at this level. I refer to this process as taking apart the box and reconstructing it.

Examples of service reconstruction abound at R-Arc. In one example we closed a group home, and reinvested traditional resources into a variety of uniquely designed living arrangements. In other situations we have "decoupled" just a slice of the budget and staffing from a group home to support a person in his or her own apartment. Navigating the process of reinvesting traditional resources into individualized supports takes a degree of mastery. Staff must be skilled in financial, human resource, and regulatory requirements in addition to having the capacity to enact a person-centered design. A reinvestment of decoupled resources helped Maryanne get her own apartment within walking distance of some of her favorite places, like the new Dinosaur Barbecue in Troy. Living in her apartment has improved Maryanne's psychological well-being. Once on an intense regiment of psycho-active medications, Maryanne now manages well without any drugs at home or at work. Coming from an institution and then a group home, for the first time Maryanne identifies her apartment as her own place. She now challenges staff if they don't call her first before coming over – a small but personally empowering gesture.

The organizational task of creating changes in practice to achieve Level 1-2 individualization of supports is often one of re-engineering the existing supports into new configurations. The task of reaching for Level 2-3 depends on the capacity of the organization and government agencies to support and encourage innovation. New forms of support require a more flexible use of government dollars, along with intentional harvesting of the natural resources of people with disabilities, their families, and communities and direct support staff. Support arrangements that draw heavily on natural resources are inevitably more creative and original, requiring a different type of organizational approach and form. Beyond individual, team and organizational capacity, an appropriate financial platform, e.g. one that is not based on fifteen-minute increments of service, is crucial to sustain an individualization supports orientation.

The Connection of Innovation to Individualized Supports

We move into the territory of innovation if the support we are offering to assist an individual achieve a valued outcome is new to our practice. More innovative approaches are personally and organizationally exciting as the thrill of breaking new ground infects all those who are involved. This "newness" typically calls for changes in organizational structures, practices, and processes, including modifications to administrative functions: finance, human resources, and corporate compliance. Perhaps the strongest indicators of social innovation are partnerships with individuals and families, community engagement, and personal development. Does power and

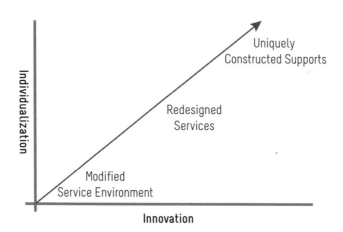

INNOVATION AND INDIVIDUALIZED SUPPORTS

influence move away from hierarchal power over to shared power with? Does a support arrangement significantly broaden the commitments beyond the agency to the community? On a deeper level, does the new arrangement require personal change and the challenging of core beliefs of all those involved in designing the supports?

Key Points

- The purpose of individualizing supports is to assist a person with DD to experience a typical life in natural places in the community not exclusively in program settings in ways that promote personal choice and decision making, control over one's personal space and resources, and assumption of valued roles in friendship, at work, and in their community.

- Given the continued dominance of the Institutional and Managed Care models, the development of individualized supports may need to be approached in degrees to open pathways to change, increase readiness of key stakeholders, test the assumptions of service provision, and develop mind-sets and competencies to support increased self-directed and determined life experiences in the future.

- For legacy service providers, the higher degree of individualization, the more need for an innovative approach.

Guided Self or Team Learning Journey

1. Perform *Exercise 10: How Individualized and Innovative are Your Services and Support?* (page 174). Use this exercise to identify the individualized supports and innovations in your agency. If you have one, evaluate the individualized supports project tied to this learning journey: how individualized and innovative is it?

2. Has your agency attempted to individualize supports? How so? What has worked and what has not worked?

3. How do different levels of individualization impact on personal outcomes?

4. What steps should your agency take to get to the next level of individualization?

Beth Mount's fiber art "Keys to Life" depicting
ten individualized support arrangements

10

Aligning an Organization with
Integrated and Community Supports

*It is the joy, passion, and beauty that we infuse into life that is the glory
of the human species. I think leaders can contribute to that joy –and to its
extinguishment. I think administrative memoranda should be constructed
as works of poetry, that organization charts should be exquisite pieces of
sculpture, that relations between a boss and subordinate should have the
qualities of a Balanchine ballet, that work should include immersion into a
glorious fiction.*[57]

—*James March*

*The challenge is to manage the contradictions of stability, learning and
change.*[58]

—*Edgar Schein*

An agency that offers integrated supports is flexibly designed for ongoing adaptation
of supports, negotiated roles, and innovation. These organic arrangements assume
more natural relational forms, such as an individual sharing her life with a family or
friend, or looking to a paid neighbor for support. Continual learning on individual,
team, and agency-wide levels is necessary to generate new structural forms and relationships. Creating the organizational conditions needed to extend person-centered
practices and individualized supports to an increasing proportion of people is yet
another leverage point to break free of our competing commitments. Among these
conditions is an organizational community with shared purpose and vision that encourages development and learning at all levels, an open community that deepens its
internal capacities while routinely renewing itself through positive exchanges with the
external world. This chapter examines exterior manifestations of R-Arc's commitment
to individualizing supports. These designs are visible artifacts of our culture and our
leaders' interior condition.

Creating Blue Space In Our Organizations

Aligning with integrated supports is contingent upon creating blue spaces, wherein
we honestly assess our selves and try new things. In this safe container, we creatively

design our leap from legacy services to integrated and then community supports. Blue spaces allow us to move beyond simple problem solving to act on the intention of facilitating right relationships, learning, and innovation. It is the integration of blue space opportunities into everyday practice that makes learning a normative part of an agency's culture, and allows for support innovations that benefit growing numbers of people. R-Arc aspires to enact, yet has not fully realized, a person-centered friendly status. Moving towards a learning orientation requires an appreciation of what gives life in our organization, rather than an exclusive focus on what is going wrong. Building upon our positive core comes out of a will to construct our own reality.

The Journey to a Learning Organization

R-Arc leadership has intentionally worked to develop an organizational community of positive relationship and learning since the late 1980s. Informed by our appreciative cultural gene and our ongoing practice of organization development, we moved with determination to build good relational form and learning into three levels of our agency – individual, team, and organizational. As I drew richly from my professional training and educational background to inform my various leadership roles with R-Arc, organization development became the primary strategy in creating an agency with person-centered capacities. Organization Development (OD) is defined as:

> …*a system-wide and values-based collaborative process of applying behavioral science knowledge to the adaptive development, improvement, and reinforcement of such organizational features as the strategies, structures, processes, people, and cultures that lead to organizational effectiveness.*[59]

Early OD proponents[60] had heavy humanistic leanings; they believed that organizations exist to serve human as opposed to corporate needs. OD strategies aimed at ensuring that the fit was right between the individual employee and the organization included the development of positive work climates and meaningful job designs. The humanistic side of OD resonated with our leadership, given R-Arc's appreciative culture. Starting in the early 1980s, I functioned as the internal R-Arc OD person. I partnered with our external OD consultant, Dr. Nancy Howes (as described in Chapter 3) to implement ways to improve our work community.

During this time, R-Arc attempted a variety of OD methods such as strategic planning, team building, climate analysis surveys, interdepartmental conflict resolution, survey feedback projects, structural re-engineering, finance, compliance and human resource systems development, work and job redesign, and at least one shot at Total Quality Management, a practice of management focused on obtaining high customer satisfaction by continuously improving products and services.

Strategic planning became a way to engage and enhance our R-Arc community, and helped to create the conditions for organizational learning. Prior to our first planning efforts in the 1980s, R-Arc consisted of loosely coupled departments and programs reflecting service functions (residential and day) or target populations (adults or children) with little or no overarching strategy or consciously shared vision. This divisional structure generated subcultures located in residential, day and children services, which further divided the agency with varying assumptions about the usefulness of group services or the ascendancy of clinicians over direct care workers. A seminal strategic planning process that unfolded over a good part of 1988 set the stage for a cohesive strategic thrust towards person-centered practices and innovative supports. We began with multiple meetings at the program level, given the lack of a strong administrative core to knit the divisions together. After a year of dispersed planning efforts, we migrated to meetings consisting of a representative cross-section of the agency from the Board of Directors to people supported. This provided a container for dialogue, helped to make sense of our world, and integrated visions across all R-Arc divisions. Out of the protracted discussions emerged our first set of unified strategic agreements. They were:

- Promoting opportunities for more integrated work and living settings for persons with developmental disabilities.
- Providing new innovative service modes by developing ongoing demonstration projects.
- Reducing our segregated services and programs.
- Generating new resources to support increased community integration of persons with developmental disabilities.
- Promoting R–Arc cause and mission through clearer, more effective communication.

Our strategic plan effectively pulled our loosely coupled programs together under a dominant value orientation. This orientation, which continues to this day in an evolved form, resulted in activities to limit the size of residential living settings to three people, produced part-time community volunteer opportunities for people served in our day treatment center, and a few years later led to the downsizing of our work center and the creation of the Community Inclusion Project, one of the first of its kind in New York State.

Another result of this strategic planning effort was the intentional use of participatory organization development methods. These methods were based on action learning cycles, a precursor to the learning organization. For example, we used a highly collaborative process called Future Search Conference to kick off the work center redesign initiative. Following the prototypical Future Search agenda, a three day meeting brought together individuals, families, R-Arc employees, representatives from state and local government, and community members to discover common ground and next steps to transform vocational services for individuals served in our work center. The Future Search Conference planning method was a particularly synergistic choice to engage our key stakeholders, because not only did it have deep roots in organization development, but it had also informed the initial design of some forms of person-centered planning for people with developmental disabilities.

The structure and facilitation of the Future Search Conference provided our conflicted R-Arc community the blue space to work free of the competing commitments of the work center downsizing project described in chapter 6. A shared vision and a proposal was created to decrease the number of people served in the work center by transitioning 20 people to supported employment and another 40 people to the Community Inclusion Project (involving over half of the individuals formerly served by the work center). This proposal was presented to then OMRDD Commissioner Elin Howe, who, along with our Board of Directors, green-lighted the project.

The success of the1988 strategic plan resulted in a preferred leadership process that involved setting direction along with coalescing and mobilizing staff to action. The shape and tools of the actual planning sessions to engage our community morphed over time and now include high-participation OD methods to foster dialogue and collaborative action such as Open-Space Technology, Appreciative Inquiry and World Café. All these methods reflect a learning organization fit and feel and play a large role in evolving R-Arc's appreciative culture. [61]

On a group level, team building and learning developed our relational maturity. One of the first team-based OD efforts was held in the early 1980s, when Nancy Howes facilitated our first cross-agency mid-manager event. The day was focused on developing agreements on role conception, expectations, acceptance, and behavior. Our interest in promoting effective and positive working relationships across and within units in the organization became the template for numerous team building sessions held at all levels and departments within the agency. Improving team performance relied on identifying goals, surfacing issues, and developing functional agreements in blame-free environments with the aid of a facilitator. By the mid-1990s, we were importing the learning organization discipline labeled "team learning" into our team development practices. With this, we were attempting to bring the group conversation to the dialogic level, a level at which team members authentically share their typically hidden assumptions and genuinely inquire about each other's thought process. In other words, we aspired to function as reflective and critical thinkers in pursuit of generative solutions.

As we enter the new century, R-Arc actively creates learning containers, or what Ed Schein[62] refers to as "culture-free islands," socially safe forums that are designed to free employees from the coercive nature of organizational norms. We have assembled communities of practice that address individualized supports, supervision, ethics, leadership, and a variety of other interest areas. Similarly, we have constructed a process to get to know a person we assist at deeper levels by taking "deep dives," guided by Theory U.[63] Deep Dives involve creating the blue space for a person's circle of support to surface and suspend their assumptions about the individual and to critically look at our support practices in terms of what is working and what is not. As with all 'U" processes, it entails a movement into emphatic understanding and a release of ego in favor of a unified outcome. One such deep dive helped a parent and his daughter's circle of support unlock from an ethical dilemma:

*A parent was struggling with a health care decision for his daughter that
had significant pros and cons regarding a complicated medical procedure involving the reversal of a colostomy bag. The daughter relied on her father to
make all her health care decisions given her lack of ability in this area. The
primary reason supporting a reversal of the colostomy was that this procedure would potentially bring his daughter back to normal functioning. The
reversal procedure was not risk free and it would require a long and trying
recovery period, which the daughter would have great difficulty adjusting
to given her low tolerance for restrictions (and there would be many) and
severe behavioral disorder. Staying with status quo would mean continuing
with daily routines involving intimate personal care that some direct care
workers had issues with performing, leading them to ask for a reassignment
to other individuals. Interestingly enough the daughter was adjusting to
these care routines. In addition, the colostomy bag had the side benefit of
preventing embarrassing accidents, which at times occurred in public places.
It was highly likely that reversing the colostomy would increase the chances
of the incontinence to reoccur. Some advocated for making his daughter
"whole again." Others pointed out that his daughter was doing well with a
prosthetic device and had already gone through one too many surgeries and
rehabs. The parent was stuck in an ethical dilemma and reached out to us
for help. We offered to facilitate an ethical decision-making session. Taking
the "deep dive," we created a safe container to explore this tough situation in
a nonjudgmental environment. With his daughter's circle of support present,
we identified all the supporting facts, observations, values, and assumptions
on both sides of the dilemma. With full understanding of both decision
pathways, we considered the resources at hand and worked to find a hybrid,
win-win solution. Thanks to the dialogical process of the deep dive, we were
able to locate a beneficial solution. Her circle of support and the parent
elected to not to reverse the colostomy, but with a renewed commitment to
safely increase her autonomy in spite of her need for on-going personal care.
A few years have gone by, and by all reports, she is happy and doing well.*

Other communities of practices have been formed to increase the capacity of direct
support professionals to connect individuals to valued roles. Two examples, both
developed by Beth Mount come to mind. *Everyday Heroes* is a facilitated developmental program that orients a direct support professional to the best ways to connect
a person with a developmental disability to community and *Lives of Distinction*, a
holistic framework that aids in discovering valued roles and community membership
for individuals. R-Arc applies these and other strategies to sensitize direct support
workers to the journey of people with developmental disabilities. I am aware of the
ongoing efforts of supervisors in our agency to connect a new staff member to the
person first before clinical records fog the support relationship. A role for support
emerges as a heart-felt relationship within a context afforded by the Lives of Distinc-

tion framework. With a heightened awareness of the person and the possibilities, the delicacy of the helping relationship can be navigated, notwithstanding that many of the people R-Arc supports present with deeply personal and troubled histories.

Developing an Ambidextrous Agency

Despite all of our success, only paying attention to the creation of innovative supports during the last fifteen years is asking for trouble. The demand for compliance with ever-expanding regulations has intensified. A larger annual budget and an increase in the numbers of employees, coupled with the need to process reams of information and perform maintenance and upkeep on multiple physical locations, have forced us to develop management systems at many levels to survive as an organization. Our previous attention focused on all things human was now captured by almost anything technically oriented to address these administrative issues. In late 1990s and early 2000s the concept of the ambidextrous organization[64] informed our leadership practices.

Prior to developing ambidextrous capacities, our organization development practices were mostly focused on the human side of managing R-Arc, attending to the fit between our agency and our employees with the purpose of building a socially adept work community. Employees provided the ideas, talent, and energy, and the agency offered wages, career, and a positive work setting. However, as we increasingly became aware of the world's many complexities, it became clear that power and politics, symbolic acts, and structural design had significant impact on our agency as well. We needed to expand our management repertoire to address these perspectives. "The challenge" as Edgar Schein said, "is to manage the contradictions of stability, learning and change." Our task was to impart a learning sensibility in all aspects of our work, from the mundane to inspirational, from the human to the technical, from stability to innovation.

Being embedded in a Medicaid-saturated environment with its medical-modeled, highly prescriptive culture, we need to address and integrate the conflicting values of a flexible work design while retaining some of the stable structures of our legacy organization. This mostly relates to managing finances, compliance, property, and risk, along with the technical aspects of creating new support arrangements. As our agency receives almost all its revenue from services provided and billed in the Medicaid program, much of our administrative process is prescribed and fixed to legacy service forms. Conflicting values of flexibility and stability can confuse staff and create disruptive energies that operate against our efforts to sustain our organization when flexibility and stability are perceived as divergent paths or either/or agendas. Embracing the notion that innovation serves the interest of stability, and stability serves the interest of innovation can aid in the reconciliation of these contradictions. An effective dance with these two forces can promote sustainability, best illustrated by the yin/yang symbol.

> *Yin and Yang, is used to describe how polar opposites or seemingly contrary forces are interconnected and interdependent in the natural world, and how they give rise to each other in turn. Opposites thus only exist in relation to each other. Yin and yang are not opposing forces (dualities), but complementary opposites, unseen (hidden, feminine) and seen (manifest, masculine), that interact within a greater whole, as part of a dynamic system.*
>
> *—Wikipedia*

Many organizations ignore, and therefore sacrifice, either stability or, more commonly, flexibility. Wildly and irresponsibly dreaming up new support forms without managing human resource, financial, and regulatory concerns is a recipe for organizational instability. Paying attention only to internal control systems leads to a petrified organizational state. In the frame of yin/yang, the stable features of an organization must, in turn, support innovative activities to ensure that the organization adapts and evolves towards its vision.

We recognize that in today's world, and into the future, our agency must effectively address the tensions of all the poles of the competing values framework –addressing control and stability while being flexible and generative in practice– in order to implement Integrative Supports in a world of multiplying regulations. Our agency's DNA delicate balance has an innovation gene as well as a stability gene by maintaining internal integrity while tapping the world outside our boundaries for learning and renewal.

Developing Individual Capacity for Person-Centered Work

At R-Arc we see each employee as a potential initiator and responder in the quest for individualized supports. As a high-leverage condition, developing and enacting leadership across all fields of our agency seems to have substantial impact on R-Arc's ability to engender a learning culture. Shared leadership refers to the maturity of employees at all levels in the organization to participate in acts of leadership, especially within their area of expertise and responsibility. It means that everyone contributes to solution generation and evolving services to individualized supports. Our philosophy of learning and generative community relates to our supports and our workplace and is enacted through our values that are consistently applied to employees as well as the people we support.

Chapter Seven on Self as an Instrument for Change makes the point that personal work is a critical factor in transforming legacy services. Acknowledging this, R-Arc works at developing individual capacity for generative learning and person-centered work, deep and wide in our organization. On a person-by-person level, we invest a lot of time developing our attitudes, beliefs and self-awareness to move the integrated and community agenda forward. However, leadership development is done not in the traditionally prescriptive way. A common view of leaders is that they are an elite group of higher-ups in control and with all the answers. We understand that direct support employees are at the heart of the organization and thus, have valuable insights. By definition the leap to the Supports Models is to an emerging yet not fully known state, made primarily through the "heart work" of direct care workers. Therefore, there are no "experts" that can tell us what to do. This leads to the following conclusions:

Shared leadership aligns with integrated supports, Personal development strategies are necessary to build individual flexibility and mastery to work within organically emergent support arrangements, and intentionally created blue spaces are critical to promote personal and organizational capacity to effectively function during times of high anxiety and change.

How can one prepare for leading in times of transformative change? At R-Arc, we see the need for leaders who are self-aware, motivated by social change, relationally competent, action-oriented, and able to rise above the emotional fray. R-Arc leaders must be ambidextrous, working with both innovation and stability agendas. They must be able to function within the rules on one hand, where life is perceived as a series of discrete encounters with winners or losers, and on the other hand to be able to creatively "keep the game in play," in a world of turmoil and uncertainty.[65] As instruments of change, leaders function comfortably with the yin/yang quality of duality as they engage in a social action learning cycle (see chapter 12). The question then becomes how to build a critical mass of people with these capacities the organization. In the blue spaces, people are achieving self-mastery and the organization is learning and experimenting with new forms of support. Following is a look at how R-Arc has developed the capacity of its members.

Approaching Employee Development

We are conceptually clear about our own development; however, we struggle with how to socialize new employees to our agency values, mission, vision, and work orientation, and are in a constant process of revising our employee development activities. We painstakingly examine the messages sent to our organizational community, and find it a challenge to operate outside a hierarchical position. This is especially the case when much of the workforce expects direction to come from those in positions of authority. Ultimately, we would like to operate completely from a partnership-based orientation. However, we own up to the fact that our interactions are not always mutual or respectful: we are very much a work in progress.

As the agency is seeking good form as a provider, our organizational members are also developing personally. Designing development strategies to foster the emotional intelligence of others is a complex undertaking. So is shifting the perception of employees to attend to yin/yang qualities in the flow of their daily work. We often wonder whether we can, as formal agency leaders, directly affect an employee's emotional development or perceptual center. I have observed that there is no direct line between what we do and how an employee develops. Therefore, we choose to work on creating nurturing learning environments rather than looking for motivational schemes to manipulate employee learning. A primary example of this is how we facilitate the employee socialization process as a newly hired person enters the organization. Reflected in these examples is the blue space concept, i.e., the creation of a learning and growth container with features of safety and challenge designed into the process.

Socializing the New Employee to Our Culture

At our best we attempt to understand each employee's personal orientation to the work and the world. As new employees enter our agency, we assist them in making the connection between inspirational sources in their life and their work supporting individuals at R-Arc. From day one, a message is conveyed through agency documents, new employee trainings, and most importantly by our supervisors that this is a place to contribute in unique and meaningful ways and grow as a person. If the new employee is open to this message, the experience can be life altering. One of the primary social mediums to build commitment to R-Arc goals and purpose is the supervisor-employee relationship.

Supervisors are charged with helping employees have clarity about R-Arc purpose and strategic interests, develop personal mastery on the job, extend their influence in their organizational community, and feel appreciated for their contributions. Acting in the role of a coach, the supervisor helps the employee locate their voice in their work, which emanates from their personal history and value system. Assisting employees tune into their voice is often done intuitively, but can be facilitated with the use of personal assessment tools, such as the Myers-Briggs Personality Types Inventory, the Thomas-Kilman Conflict Survey, Kolb's Learning Styles Inventory, and other related instruments. These tools can provide valuable information about how we perceive and enact our personality type, values, and beliefs in our world. Understanding personal difference may also help to develop an appreciative relational climate, one that aligns with person-centeredness. It is one of our core assumptions that employees who practice self-mastery better understand person-centered dynamics, and can participate more readily in enlightened relationships. To this end we have implemented numerous ways to engage employees in this process through trainings and coaching sessions. Some samples of this include staff development initiatives we call Accelerated Leadership (a self-guided development process with readings and interviews with organizational members) and Corporate University.

Corporate University

Our agency's Corporate University Program best represents our approach to engaging employees in self-development. The term is lifted from a corporate practice of partnering with colleges and universities to deliver courses in a variety of areas to "skill up" their employees by increasing the depth and scope of employee training with the introduction of college level courses given on site or at a university. Our Corporate University Program has taken curricula from an Antioch Masters in Management program, with its complimentary values of practical application and theory, and incorporated it into supervisory development. The ingredients of this program include five full days of classroom instruction designed around self-assessment and management theory with topic areas including: learning styles, personal effectiveness, emotional intelligence, role intentionality, performance management, interpersonal communication, managing difference, positive discipline and team development. Other mini-learning sessions are offered as well, with subjects varying from Social Role Valorization (SRV) to time management. Classroom instruction is reinforced through a mentorship arrangement and on the job practical support from a supervisor. Each student develops their own learning agreement, with chosen goals related to personal and supervisory development which the mentor and supervisor co-sign and design strategies to support the employee. Past learners have found the sessions with a mentor especially helpful in applying frameworks learned in the class to discussions related to real situations at work. All of this is implemented within an appreciative frame of reference.

R-Arc's twist on a Corporate University includes developing each employee's capacity to become a reflective practitioner who pursues personal mastery by understanding self and others, and acts intentionally in service of a defined purpose and practice. Kolb's learning style model, which describes a cycle of acting, reflecting, theorizing and applying, expresses the process of the reflective practitioner. At an individual employee level, it means shifting one's perspective, getting out of one's skin, and moving to situations that offer the potential of fresh learning and creating, to shed an either/ or worldview.

R-Arc Accelerated Leadership process, another facilitated development initiative, also seeks to do the same, by introducing new employees to our values and supports orientation through readings and interviews with organizational members. In this learning process, employees get a strong dose of where we come from and where we are going. These shifts of perception, knowledge, and action prepare employees for the change journey to Integrated and Community Supports.

Opening Our Organizational Boundaries to New Ideas and Taking our Vision of Individualized Supports to the World.

We have always understood that we are responsible to join with others in creating our world, based on a belief that our actions help to maintain or evolve the system that supports persons with developmental disabilities. Therefore, we strongly believe that it is critical to interact with our relevant environment to promote our social justice agenda, a core value imprinted on our agency by our highly active founding board members Henrietta Messier and Ellie Pattison. They were consummate systems advocates, challenging status quo, influencing policy direction, organizing social action, and building community. Compared with other local non-profit organizations, our interaction frequency with entities at the local, state, and federal level was off the map. External engagement is more about enacting our environment as opposed to participating in the competitive market place and ranges from political activism to environmental scanning. We also make ourselves available to participate in policy forum discussions at the state and local governmental levels. Ultimately, as a result of this we are often asked to assume leadership roles in provider associations and local government community boards.

> *In the mid-1990's, state funding for Family Supports services was on the chopping block. Henrietta and John Fudjak, our Director of Family Supports at that time, organized families throughout New York State into an advocacy coalition. The ad-hoc family coalition engaged in educational activities targeted at legislators and others that eventually led to budget restorations for Family Supports services. One of our successes in this realm arrived when as a result of the strong advocacy efforts led by our agency, Family Supports funding became "the third rail" in the New York State budget process, meaning it was off the budget-cutting table in the minds of the Governor and Legislature.*

Of equal impact to R-Arc's organizational development was our constant engagement in learning exchanges. Over the years, our boundaries have been open to the teachings of mentors, consultants, and peers from other agencies to explore alternative ways of designing and operating an organization. We also traveled far and wide, in person and by teleconference, to learn from others in their communities or at professional conferences. Learning journeys that take us to places of potential have informed our practice in many ways. We have also contributed to the learning of others by inviting and welcoming fellow travelers in their quest to learn about individualized supports. When the spirit moved us, we presented what we have learned at conferences throughout the country.

Though we have participated in more learning and practice communities than we can remember there are two that stand out: Shared Living community of practice and the Learning Institute on Innovation on Individualized Supports –both coordinated by the New York State Association of Community and Residential Agencies (NYSA-CRA). R-Arc staff provided considerable time and expertise to both of these efforts. For the Learning Institute on Innovation, I partnered with Beth Mount as a co-designer and faculty for the Learning Institute for three cohort groups across New York State over a five-year period from 2007-2011. We were guided by Theory U in developing a deep learning experience for staff from the selected agencies. The institute was structured around initiatives that focused on individualizing supports for people served by the participating agencies. In the process of designing proposals to individualize services for specific people, institute participants engaged in reflective personal learning, team development, and learning journeys that took them to organizations with innovative practices. The institute shifted the perspectives of the participants and seeded some of the agencies with individualized practices. The institute played a small part in fueling the fires of individualized supports in DD policy making by creating blue space for new thinking and practice.

Another significant external collaboration was our involvement in the Think Tank on Individualized Supports, which had an impact on New York State policy on DD service orientation. The purpose statement of the Think Tank, to which we contributed, is:

> *The Individualized Supports Think Tank is an independent group of self-advocates, parents, providers, and others committed to increasing opportunities for individualized supports in New York State. The primary activity of the Think Tank is to create a learning community around the concept of individualized supports. With the belief that knowledge is power, the Think Tank will study and research promising best practices, ideas, and funding methods. The Think Tank will also examine New York State and national experiences and examples of individualized supports for people with developmental disabilities.*

Our engagement with others external to our organization is critical to our ongoing process of renewal. Without importing (and exporting) new perceptions, practices, and people, we believe we will become passive victims of a dying system. Our engagements are frequent and reciprocal with other organizations and people, receiving as much as we give with our partners outside the boundaries of our agency. In the final analysis, our renewal and innovations come as much from our interior (personal and organizational) as from the exterior world.

Is the Ecosystem Person-Centered Friendly?

There are numerous variables that have a significant impact on our ability to be successful in providing Integrated and Community Supports. Given that our agency is situated in a series of nested environments –from our local community to the field of DD providers to the national scene– the ability to enact these types of supports does not exclusively sit with R-Arc. In many ways, our involvement with the Medicaid program intensifies our competing commitments and inhibits our evolutionary momentum as New York State legitimizes the Institutional Model in its laws and regulations. As managed care fever spreads across the country, concerns surface as the Managed Care Model installs new payment and coordination machinery imported from health care to the DD System. Managed care creates structures and processes that some believe will be corporately driven, twice removed from the partnerships we have with individuals. An example of this is the coordination function, though labeled "person-centered" coordination often operates within a deficit-based medical framework. Aligning our organizational forms to the managed care world will confound our agency's ability to co-design individualized supports.

There is much in the world of institutional care that has created the conditions that dampen innovation and close blue space. The legacy system, and all its architecture, is designed to get client – and consumer-related outcomes, not citizen outcomes. Therefore, a system designed to produce and regulate legacy services is not set up for personalization. Inherent in the Institutional and Managed Care Model is a mandate for standardization and efficiency that works against our ability to uniquely respond to individual circumstance and make the best use of all available resources. Furthermore, these models of care are implemented from a power over command and control model of management, which suppresses mutual exchanges between providers and individuals. The best that is achieved is a form of paternalism, a caring that reflects the parent/child relationship. Maybe we can customize on the edges, but the provider-consumer relational form is retained.

Even without these contextual constraints, we as individuals and organizations come largely underdeveloped and unprepared for the relational demands of the most evolved support forms. Most of us struggle in our personal lives to break out of the hierarchical mode even with our most intimate relationships. We work in pyramidal organizations with divisional structures compartmentalizing day and residential services that direct activities from on-high. While this may fit with the objectives of an institutional model, it stymies person-centered innovation.

Perhaps re-imaging traditional organizational structures as more organic forms will free up some blue space in our workplaces. If we apply a playful metaphor to organizational design it may help us envision different organizational forms to promote innovation.[66] For example, as an alternative to the image of an organization as a pyramid or a machine, picture it as a parent spider plant sending out and nurturing stems and buds of individualized support prototypes. If they catch root, they may sprout on-going support arrangements for people. This more organic organizational image suggests a re-orientation of how we manage. We grow and nurture spider plants, in contrast, we structurally shore up pyramids with stable, rigid structures; or re-engineer machines to make the gears mesh better. Spider plant arrangements may be the kind of organizational form to more appropriately align with person-centered practices, revealing a wide gap to cross from institutional care to community supports. This sounds awfully critical, but the fact is that many of our social institutions –educational, health care, and religious organizations– reflect mechanical and hierarchical qualities. Organizations from a variety of sectors are largely coming from the same place and same mind-set, and all have sustainability issues. The institutional form is a dying organizational entity, increasingly out of touch with individuals and citizenship outcomes. Managed care is merely a transitional strategy to address coordination, cost and resource allocation and mostly ignores larger questions of sustainability and the support of people in valued social roles.

Those interested in moving towards Integrated and Community Supports Models are distracted from creating more flexible organizational forms as they retool to survive in an increasingly controlled managed care environment. Given this, there is a real threat that it will grow so difficult to open up blue space that the shift from Care to Support will stall indefinitely. Yet the reality of today's world is "it is what it is." We exist within a dominant care model as opposed to a support model. The challenge is how to get a DD system to support people, as opposed to the people being servants to a system. Our energies must continue to maintain some equilibrium while we create organizational forms that can produce authentic individualized supports. Our interest is to bring forth a good organizational form that builds a meaningful community, a place where employees and key stakeholders are fully engaged and where efforts are made to support people in valued citizenship based roles. Perhaps its time to decorate our office windows with spider plants to remind us of the forms our agencies must take to be friendly to person-centered work.

Functioning as a Learning Organization

Our work around aligning our organization to integrated work takes shape on the individual, team, organizational, and external engagement levels. In many ways, we have put into practice Peter Senge's concept of learning architecture, which refers to a social structure that promotes deep learning and action. This deep learning is worked at the individual and organizational level by aligning our awareness and sensibilities, our attitudes and beliefs, and our skills and capacities with person-centered practices. Personal and organizational development is carried out within the framework of our guiding ideas and strategic directions. Our communities of learning and practice are informed by organization development theory, methods and tools.

On a good day, we fire on all cylinders with a generative practice that encourages wonderful supports innovation; other days we lean towards the mainstream of an institutional, legacy-based environment. Ultimately, we are seeking a balance that allows our agency to fire on all cylinders. The end stage looks more like a constant re-generating cycle rather than a linear project management plan with its end point fully defined before the journey begins. I believe that blue space is widened by the attitudes, beliefs, and self-awareness of R-Arc leadership and employees and their ability to foster relationships based on caring and collaboration. Our vision of community and citizenship for all people informs our evolutionary direction. Our ambidextrous skills and capacities, along with processes and practices that engender learning and innovation, keep our organization viable as we move towards Integrated and Community Support Models.

These are the conditions to bring forth a future of possibilities while maintaining some degree of organizational stability. Each provider agency, being a contained human community, organically creates its own conditions that nurture person-centered practices and valued outcomes for the people they support. Yet, R-Arc's story holds great value to inform the practices of other organizational communities.

Key Points

- Individualized supports flourish in an organizational context of generative learning and appreciation.

- Theory, methods, processes and practices of organization development help to grow an agency that is friendly to person-centered work and innovations leading to individualized supports. Organization development is a primary way to create blue space in an agency for critical thinking, challenging status quo, innovating generative solutions, nurturing personal development, and reflecting on practices.

- Given the current socio-economic and regulatory environment coupled with the demand of more individualized supports, agencies must develop an ambidextrous capacity to balance organizational stability and innovation.

- Generative capacities to support person-centered work and individualized support must be developed and operating at the individual, group, and organization wide levels.

- Organizational learning entails an internal capacity to develop and evolve as well as to open the agency and its members to new ideas, perspectives, and practices outside its boundaries.

Guided Self or Team Learning Journey

1. Answer survey questions in *Exercise 11: Person-Centered Friendly Organizational Survey* (page 176) with a peer or in the learning group. Identify what aligns with person-centered work and what does not in your agency. Discuss areas of development that may be of high leverage to help move your agency forward. What strategies has your agency employed to foster person-centered friendly organizational conditions? How ready is your organization to work on the edge of a new support form? Does your agency's leadership consciously and intentionally create (blue) space for creative solutions to emerge from collaborative practice?

2. Identify "places of potential" to visit (other people, agencies, communities outside your organization). Use *Exercise 12: Learning Journey Observational Guide* (page 183) to help structure your visits for maximum learning.

11

Developing Capacity as an Innovation Generator

Though we travel the world over to find the beautiful, we must carry it with us, or we will not find it. [67]

–*Ralph Waldo Emerson*

Something shifts on a large scale only after a period of small steps, organized around small groups patient enough to learn and experiment and learn again. [68]

–*Peter Block*

The process of innovation brings forth greater potential for effectiveness within human systems at all levels. All the care and support models possess the capacity to motivate and support the creation of something new. However, innovation is expressed differently at each evolutionary stage. In Institutional Care, the bureaucracy innovates in the administering of the system. The bureaucrat, not concerned with surfacing and challenging core assumptions, focuses on how to decrease processing time, how to manage daily schedules more effectively, and how to structure a rate or design a contract. When engaging in innovation, managed care systems are radically restructuring the accountability routines, for instance tying payments to performance-based outcomes as opposed to process-driven services. In the case of Integrated Supports, innovation occurs when support arrangements are co-created rather than delegated to the providers and services are emergent not predetermined. For Community Supports, innovation seeks to re-align the social relationships of the whole community, including beliefs, roles, and responsibilities, and thus provides a new context for offering support.

Innovations in the environments of Integrative Supports and Community Supports are distinctively social in nature. They offer people and their community new and richer ways to be and act together. R-Arc engages in innovations that meet the demands of each support model, but our primary interest has been to generate social innovation as a way to move out of the gridlock we experience from our competing commitments. In this chapter we will explore what we are learning about the nature of innovations in support models, and the process and structures that generate them.

Developing as an Innovation Generator

Developing an innovation generator[69] within a legacy agency is no easy task. Our intentional journey to a good supports form, propelled by visions of valued lives, nurtured by our appreciative culture, facilitated by reflective leaders and organizational learning structures, and enacted through partnerships with individuals and families all depend on innovation generation. Yet even with all of this, any particular try at innovative practice may fizzle out or misfire. This chapter digs deeper to look at three factors that facilitate creative action:

- Understanding the nature and focus of the innovation,
- Building organizational infrastructure to facilitate innovation and integrate new practices into the operations of the agency, and
- Letting go of our fear of change by dancing with dragons in the blue space

The Nature of Socially Innovating

If we believe that only making changes in our internal structures, processes, and practices will move us toward integrated and community supports, we are mistaken. Without realigning our relationships and consciously revising our assumptions, we will miss the mark. Innovations that produce new social arrangements, such as those that may be found in individualized supports, are quite different than those typically produced in legacy environments. This kind of newness is produced outside the typical boundaries of the defined sectors of our society, where the individual meets provider, public official, employer, and others in the blue space to tackle needs not effectively addressed by any one sector. The following definition from *The Open Book of Social Innovation* begins to get at this distinction.

> *Social innovations are new ideas (products, services and models) that simultaneously meet social needs and create new social relationships or collaborations. In other words, they are innovations that are both good for society and enhance society's capacity to act.*[70]

For our agency, social innovation starts with challenging current thinking about people with disabilities. In a truly innovative person centered approach, many of the previous social expectations and arrangements are disbanded, relieving traditional providers of their predefined roles and responsibilities. What is co-created is based on emerging beliefs about people with developmental disabilities, perceiving a "frame of capacity" rather than "deficits." If successful, what bubbles up from the blue space will have a significant impact on the greater community, not just the individual.

Innovating Within the Walls of a Legacy Service
Commitment to Innovation

Organizational commitment, resources, and active efforts to move practices from prototypes into the mainstream of organizational routines are required for social innovation. In terms of commitment, The Arc of Rensselaer County's mission statement emphasizes that our intention is to "build the capacity of the community to support citizenship of people with developmental disabilities." This was further reinforced by our most recent strategic agenda, which concretely states our intention to:

- Bring Forth Self Defined and Self Directed Capacities Using Structural and Social Innovations.
- Promote Healthy Lifestyles by Supporting Wellness and Professional Mastery.
- Build Sustainable Communities: Managing the Triple Bottom Line (Resource Viability, Civic Responsibility, and Green Orientation.)
- Engage in Continuous Improvement: Achieving Quality Individual and Organizational Outcomes.

These declarations are supported by investments of resources. Our agency has reinvested resources from legacy services to individualized supports, created an Innovation and Design Unit, promoted ongoing action learning, and created new ways to support people and families to tap into and make good use of government funds that are directly tied to self-directed supports.

Reinvesting Legacy Resources in Innovative Supports

R-Arc engagement in OMRDD's 1997 *Search for Excellence* initiative illustrates the way we use openings in the system that funds and regulates us for a significant reinvestment of legacy funding into individualized supports. In this initiative, R-Arc transitioned nine individuals from a congregate care living situation to individual supportive living environments within a cost-neutral budget. By reinvesting funds from the closure of the Prout Avenue residence, a single budget was transformed into household budgets to finance three two-person apartments and individual budgets to support three individuals in their own apartments. This was achieved by designing a process that started with a future vision for the project, team building with individuals, families, and staff, and working with The R-Arc Board and OMRDD to obtain political support for the project. This, in turn, led to redesigned work and job structures to implement individual supports rather than the institutional routines found in congregate care.

Implementing Organizational Structures Responsible for Innovation

Our investment in innovation exponentially increased in 2002, when we developed an Innovation and Design Unit. The unit, led by Sandy Van Eck, works directly with individuals and families co-designing individualized supports. A typical engagement with Sandy and her fellow innovators may be prompted by a parent who is repelled by the thought that their son or daughter will be captured by a life of eternal clienthood. This was exactly the situation when we used government funds designated for self-determination to make one family's dream come alive.

Robert's parents were at their wits end after the system failed in over fifteen different residential school placements to meet their son's needs throughout his childhood. Although Robert had exhibited many troublesome behaviors that in the past excluded him from community settings, he was now almost twenty-one and was seeking a more typical life experience. Robert's family sought out our agency based on our reputation as flexible supports designers. Right from the start, Sandy viewed Robert from a wider lens than clinicians had at the residential schools. At the initial planning meetings, Sandy saw a twenty-one year old young man who was excited about starting the next phase of his life. With that mind-set things went quite differently. Through a visioning process, it was determined that Robert wanted to live in a country setting with the ability to bike into a nearby town. He identified "working with his hands" in a job with a salary. He also expressed a desire to volunteer if it was related to his vocational interests. Another pathway he wanted to pursue was painting and woodcarving. Given this was his first independent living situation outside his family, Robert and his parents decided that a live-in mentor could provide him with the guidance, unconditional support, and reassurance he would need to be successful on his own. Part of the support arrangement included a circle of support personally selected by Robert to help manage and guide his self-directed budget and individual plan. Robert and others in his support circle acknowledged that things can and will change, and the plan and supports need to be flexible in his life journey. He currently lives in his own apartment, has a job in a state park and gets to spend his leisure time riding his bike and doing art work.

When we develop arrangements like Robert's, we are acting in service to a vision of citizenship for a person with a developmental disability by addressing the organic complexity of high individualization—not by standardization and simplification—but by moving decision making to a circle of support and support brokers or facilitators. Some liken it to a new kind of economy: one that features some of the traditional service system, but also includes the resources that come with new roles and relationships. It is seen as social innovation because it sheds the delegated service arrangement and replaces it with distributed networks to sustain and manage relationships, and the boundaries between support provider and service recipient are more permeable. It also relies on repeated interactions to plan, design, and implement supports within an ongoing partnership arrangement. As mentioned in previous chapters, the person, along with his family, play active roles in all phases of the design and implementation of supports.

Sandy's unit also functions as a consulting resource to other departments in our agency as they engage in individualization initiatives. This unit functions as a parallel structure to the programs, and focuses on innovation without operational responsibilities. Learning forums are abundant and shed light on all the aspects of an evolving support model at our agency. An appreciative organizational culture and organizational learning architecture support the innovation process as described in the chapter on aligning an organization to integrated supports. R-Arc support staff that work in the finance, compliance, and human resource departments, adjust their practices to support new and emerging support arrangements.

Promoting Innovations Through Social Action Learning

Just as the parent spider plant throws off numerous shoots, our agency has incubated many individualized supports initiatives over the years. Some have been integrated into the mainstream of our agency's support offerings such as the Community Inclusion Project discussed earlier in this book. Possessing the sensibility of a business incubator, R-Arc seeks out concepts to promote individualized arrangements. A current example was born out of a two-day learning event where the focus task was to identify and enable potential structures to grow more support arrangements that are individualized. One design involved using unencumbered resources from the various legacy programs and blending them into "seamless" supports for individuals who are interested in more self-directed opportunities. The term seamless refers to supporting an individual 24/7 in a blended support arrangement with one team as opposed to serving the person with separate teams in day habilitation and residential habilitation program silos. The idea excited us and we decided to prototype seamless services, resulting in eight new individualized support arrangements. A new team structure is in the works that will combine the supports provided to these eight people with all of the other supports R-Arc offers to self-determination arrangements. This will establish the function of supporting these arrangements in the mainstream of our agency.

This process of prototyping new individualized supports, such as seamless services, and integrating these practices into our agency's service structure reflects a social action learning cycle. Social action learning is a process enacted in partnership with individuals and families. It starts with listening for new possibilities, designing new support arrangements, discovering what works from the trials, incorporating new learning into everyday practice, and then repeating the cycle. It takes the form of ongoing tests that challenge, but do not destroy, our positive operating core. They are small experiments designed to get us unstuck from our competing commitments by challenging our assumptions about our roles and relationships with individuals, what is financially feasible, what is allowable in terms of regulations, and what support arrangement blends the appropriate amount of risk with safety.

"Transformation through conservation," is a process where a few basic features of an agency (or support model) are retained as a new generation of supports unfolds. This is where an organization clarifies what is important to conserve in the organization, often in the form of principle, purpose, and people.[71] Our experiments are risky enough to generate innovative approaches, yet small enough to keep the individual or agency out of financial, legal, or regulatory jeopardy. While some parts of our agency are innovating supports, other parts are stabilized in the traditional ways of operating. A constant flow of experimentation informs how we assist individuals and families, and then normalizes into a new way of providing support. Past innovations become stable ground for new tests. Small, low levels of individualization are occurring across all organizational departments while high levels of individualization unfold at the edges of our practice. In essence, conscious application of the social action learning cycle by R-Arc members operationalizes the structure of an evolving practice with the characteristics of the "transcend and include" cycles as described in chapter 3.

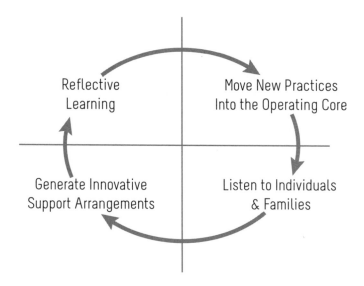

We Dance With Dragons In the Blue Space

The final move in performing a creative act is letting go. Although we can and must provide safe containers in our organization and communities for dialogue and thoughtful action, bringing forth positive futures requires a deep dive into our interior personal and collective space where we confront what limits us the most: our own fears about change. As we create new support practices, the proverbial beast is provoked. We are knocked off our center as we move into unknown territory without the anchor of our legacy services. Otto Scharmer names this letting go process as "opening our will" to our highest purpose and future self.[72] This requires that we find the quiet center of our blue space so we can, as Rebecca Chan Allen says, Dance with our Dragons.[73]

In order to release our energies to function as innovation generators we must dance with our dragons, not be consumed by them. Chan Allen metaphorically characterizes dragons as the energies that exist within and outside of our self – potentially threatening on one hand and offering opportunities on the other. In Western myths dragons are conceived as monsters that can destroy, whereas in Eastern tradition dragons are creatures of universal vitality. Their energy is one of an impersonal duality that reflects both the chaos and order of our world with potentiality for destruction and creation. If we prefer the Western dragon, our mission is to go to war against the

DANCING WITH DRAGONS
Letting Go to Bring Forth Innovations

LEARNING ABOUT
Different Ways of Perceiving and
Supporting People With Disabilities

INTEGRATING
Support Arrangements
in Agency Operations

LISTENING TO
Individuals and Families Experiencing
Different Support Arrangements

CO-DESIGNING
and Implementing Supports
with Individuals and Families

DANCING WITH DRAGONS
Letting Go of Legacy Roles and Investments

CONNECTING WITH
Visions of a Diverse Community

(Inspired by Scharmer 2007 and Chan Allen, 2002)

forces of evil. If we look to Eastern tradition, we participate in our world by dancing with our dragons. I believe that opening our will to a higher purpose and future self is more about dancing with our dragons, an approach where we engage as opposed a react.

In the course of a typical day, regardless of whether we are in the middle of a supports transformation, we experience the swirl of order and chaos. The turmoil of the human condition manifests in the struggles over resources, the controlling actions of others (government and otherwise), the diversity of cultural world views, the nature of our economic systems and social conditions, and more particular to us, the structures of the dominant DD service model. This turmoil is also present within our self, and is deeply embedded in our human psychology. These divergent energies are of the universe, an integral part of what it means to be human. If we battle them, we are merely denying a piece of ourselves; dance with them, and we can use the energy productively.

Dancing with dragons recognizes the importance of the dual function of chaos and order. Engaging in a transformative process such as the move to integrated supports can provoke controlling or unconstrained responses in the system. Too much of one versus the other can invoke the shadow of dysfunction. All of us have seen how the over-controlling, over-organized system is unresponsive to difference, creates dependency in its members, and lacks an adaptive capacity to deal with changing conditions in the environment. These systems tend to exercise power over others. The daily experience of an over-organized system is dominated by a nearly obsessive focus on compliance and paperwork in response to government regulatory controls.

Creative forces have a shadow side, as too much chaos is also destructive. Under-organized systems exhibit unfocused actions, ongoing unresolved conflicts, an inability to achieve results, and over-stretched resources. These highly chaotic systems create conditions of stress and energy dissipation, leaving no capacity to bring an innovation into practice. The most dysfunctional manifestations of both over-and under-organized systems exhibit the social plagues of prejudice, incompetence, and aggressive behavior. People in these systems often act in socially controlling and defensive ways, thereby blocking and distracting efforts to evolve more functional forms of relationships, supports and organizational design. Both kinds of systems can fall prey to personally driven, ego-hooked people hell-bent on their agenda to change the system. It is unproductive to argue for complete flexibility or total control. These are forces that must be balanced by constantly adjusting for a functional degree of organization and creativity, a chaordic capacity[74] (an organizational characteristic that blends chaos and order).

On the psychic side, dancing with dragons refers to tapping into energies present within. With this strategy, we avoid creating our own personal hell of self-deprecation or by avoiding and denying present aspects of ourselves that don't seem to fit with our self-image. We may fear losing a role we are comfortable with or our livelihood because a legacy service is being closed. We may feel threatened because we believe that individualized supports draws resources away from current services, thereby compromising the fiscal integrity of our agency. Or we might be dogmatic about our intentions to create social change, ignoring people for the principle. We can become caught up in an image of ourselves as hero liberators and lose the true mission. Dancing with dragons allows us to surface our fears, and acknowledge them through a witnessing perspective. We disarm our negative energies rather than aiming to kill them. When we expand our internal blue space, we tap into a spirit present beyond our ego. We become free to test our assumptions, without judgment, about our roles, practice, and relationships. Our future self is birthed here, and this self has the capacity to create new social arrangements.

Outside ourselves, the legacy system demands our attention with ongoing questions of sustainability, regulatory compliance, and system-wide responses to abuse events. Individuals and organizations, tested to the limits, may become reactive, exhausted from the innovation challenge and then shut down. These are challenges that cannot be addressed by seeking control, but by letting go and surrendering to the unknown. What is it truly like to operate in the blue space, the source of our creativity while controlling and chaotic energies swirl around us? Much of this book concerns moving our self and our agency into a space where co-creating supports with individuals and families is possible, seeing each voice as a knowledgeable contribution with varying offerings to a greater purpose. This chapter is about climbing up the right side of Scharmer's U after we have moved away from identification with role and services to deep purpose and future potential. Here we are acting as vessels of future change, taking our visions of social change into actionable prototypes, and sustainable forms of individualized supports.

From Fossil Fuels to Renewable Energy

Ring the bells that still can ring
Forget your perfect offering
There is a crack in everything
That's how the light gets in.

—*Leonard Cohen*

We recognize that transformational change is in order, yet our competing commitments paralyze us. How do we bring forth the new and innovative without disrupting support arrangements for a largely vulnerable population, some who are satisfied with the delegated arrangement? At times as a legacy agency CEO, I can relate to the plant manager of the largest coal burning power plant serving as the primary energy provider for an east coast urban center. Even though he is aware of the negative environmental impact of burning fossil fuel, the manager believes that shutting down the coal-burning plant without an alternative energy delivery system in place would create a disaster. Our question is, how can we engender ongoing learning within an operating entity that people and families count on until a tipping point is reached and social innovation becomes the new normative practice? The answer lies in part with an ambidextrous capacity to balance stability with innovative action. Another place to look is to our own interior condition so we become instruments of change. Lastly, we need to develop an ecosystem that nurtures integrated and community support models. The blue space must be available at the individual, organizational, and societal levels to hold and protect our newly generated vital social forms as a gardener would nurture the seedling plant.

Key Points

- Legacy agencies need to develop a capacity to generate innovation, if interested and motivated, to create individualized supports.

- Individualizing supports requires social innovation, which is the realignment of individual, family, provider, and community roles and relationships to work within and outside defined sectors of our society.

- Becoming an innovation generator requires dedicated organizational resources, defined structures and roles charged with innovation, and a personal capacity to "dance with dragons" – our internal fears and desires that can destroy or enable us.

Guided Self or Team Learning Journey

1. Reflect on the edge or type of innovation expressed in your agency! What does it look like?

2. Who are the innovators in your organization? How does the organization treat them?

3. How do your stability functions support your innovative edge? How do you manage disruptive change?

4. Perform *Exercise 13: Letting Go and Dancing with Our Dragons* (page 186). Use this as a culminating exercise to reflect on this self/team guided learning journey. Have you traveled further down the evolutionary path of individualizing supports, do you sense a new calling or a future waiting to be born? What steps will you take, and in what direction?

11

Conclusion

Furthermore, we have not even to risk the adventure alone, for the heroes of all time have gone before us. The labyrinth is thoroughly known. We have only to follow the thread of the hero path, and where we had thought to find an abomination, we shall find a god. And where we had thought to slay another, we shall slay ourselves. Where we had thought to travel outward, we will come to the center of our own existence. And where we thought to be alone, we will be with all the world.[75]

—*Joseph Campbell*

Our individual and collective narratives continue to unfold in dynamic and unpredictable ways. Within the boundaries of our agency, each conversation holds the potential to move us closer to supporting people as citizens as opposed to caring for the clients of a system. Conversely, a single event can produce enough anxiety to create power over responses. As we have experienced, overplayed hierarchical interventions restrict life-giving relationships in favor of monitoring and controlling actions. As individuals, organizations, and government agencies we have a choice to facilitate movement towards enlightened support practices or retrench to the heydays of the institutional model. Do we believe that people with developmental disabilities are citizens that can have a full life? Or do we act on the untested assumption that people with developmental disabilities are so vulnerable and generally incompetent that they need little more than our vigilance?

By now, it is apparent that a simple, logical plan cannot ignite the kind of social action that is necessary to realize valued outcomes for people with developmental disabilities. Therefore, the question remains to be asked again and again: How can we bring forth a state of evolved practice that leads to citizenship for all persons with development disabilities? I believe the story of The Arc of Rensselaer County offers some insight into this transformative journey. Ours is a story of intentional destabilization of belief structures leading to a break from legacy service models. We have done this not only because we have discerned that current service forms are fiscally unsustainable or because a growing number of individuals and families are dissatisfied with the outcomes of our legacy services, but also because our perspective has shifted. Our learning journey has taken us to new vantage points and shown us vistas of a welcoming community with diverse members. Our narrative, about finding good form for our relationships, supports, and organization, can inform others who choose similar paths. We can't offer prescriptions; the value lies in the sensibility and wisdom embodied in how we are learning to engage our world. We hope the lessons we learned in our journey can act as a philosophical guide for inspired others who choose to walk similar paths.

This wisdom is embedded in the ever-emerging culture of R-Arc and is apparent when our shared leadership generates social innovations: forms of relationship and organization that promote both self-determination and healthy community. When we are at our best, we respond to the call of the hero's journey by taking the U shaped route: going to the highest mountains to appreciate the complex landscape we must traverse, and down into the valley of our interior being to find new forms. We challenge one another to develop ourselves as leaders so that we can better see and act effectively in a complex world. Our purpose is to deepen our relationships and to transform our legacy of care services into individualized supports. Wisdom grows in the blue spaces we choose to create with one another. We act with the conviction that working this way will ultimately give the edge to enlightened solutions that promote healthy growth and wellbeing for all, from the individual living a valued life to the community existing in ecological balance.

We understand that getting rid of what we don't like about our current service models does not automatically get people the life they desire. To move in the right direction we must clearly see our destination and be acutely aware of our current context. Delivering Integrative Supports and Community Supports while remaining embedded in an environment organized for Institutional Care and Managed Care requires a release from gridlock. This means we see the competing commitments that bind us when we pit our goal of a diverse and healthy community against managing to survive in today's world, where service models based on prediction, command, and control struggle in a turbulent environment. It means that we need to be unflinchingly honest about where we sit in the evolution of developmental disability services. Do we recognize where and in what ways our current service models and structures are decaying? Do we know how the assumptions and practices that shape the whole DD system lock us into status quo? Do we sense an emerging support model? Can we open our minds, hearts, and wills to new vantage points from which we can see the old ways of support dying, and new models of care and support coming into being? Without a sense of the whole, when we operate from the center of our ego seeing only what concerns us individually, we run mindlessly in circles.

If our journey moves us towards good relational and structural forms, we naturally shift focus from ourselves to our organizations and then to our communities. With compassion for our community our blue space expands, allowing us to transcend old forms yet retain their positive elements. New forms of support and relationship are constructed through active engagement and dialogue with more and more partners, only emerging when we adopt an appreciative frame of reference to inquire into who we are, our historical progression, and what we deeply desire and want to contribute to our world. Without appreciation we will fall into dysfunctional forms of being and relating, a symptom of our unawareness and self-centeredness.

Our reflections about what we have learned at our agency may enlighten individuals and families, service providers, and government policy makers about good forms of support for persons with developmental disabilities. In summary, these reflections are:

Bringing forth new support forms requires different thinking.

The ability to move to new evolutionary forms of support requires changing how you think about people with disabilities, about the way supports are developed and provided, and about the nature of the community. Operating under the basic assumptions from the institutional era will get us more programs without getting valued outcomes. We must engage in a process to discover the diversity of the world from new and powerful vantage points. Increasing our awareness opens the door to surfacing and challenging the archaic assumptions we have about people with disabilities that are old and out-of-date. Thinking differently sustains the evolutionary journey forward.

Change begins with you.

There is nothing more effective than becoming the change you seek by deeply connecting with your purpose and change vision. From that deep connection with self emerges a leadership voice that can converse wisely with others attempting to transform services to supports. We must go beyond our technical skills to develop a generative capacity. Growing into a generative leader requires one to operate less as an expert and more as a facilitator of appreciative inquiry. If we are embedded in the institutional model, nothing less than a hero's journey will take us in the right direction.

Focus on deepening relationships with everyone, especially individuals and families.

Deeply listening to others allows for realignment from a power-dominated to a shared-power orientation. Trusting relationships between individuals, families, providers, and community members are at the core of the Integrated and Community Supports Models. These right relationships are based on compassion, authenticity, and mutuality of human exchange.[76] For care to transform to supports, roles and relationships must exhibit good form in contact and connection. This is a relationship based on sharing love as well as power.

The change that we are seeking is transformational therefore it is unresponsive to rational and linear solutions.

As support evolves toward Integrated and Community Supports Models, dynamic complexity increases. Not only must we manage more detail, but we need to negotiate with many stakeholders in the co-designing and co-implementing of support arrangements. Complexity lies in the diversity of the interests and the organic nature of an individualized plan to meet each person in all of their uniqueness. Complexity emerges from managing the creation of support forms whose shape and effectiveness can only be established by trial and revision, requiring the embrace of uncertainty in a system that demands predictability, compliance with current rules, and uniformity. Moving forward calls for the discernment and skills to facilitate an emerging practice while continuing to address the continuing demands of legacy services. Transformational change benefits from collaborative strategies such as Future Search Conferences, Communities of Practice, Appreciative Inquiry, World Café, Open Space Technology, and the U process journey, as opposed to traditional rational methods such as Total Quality Management or strategic planning to facilitate movement in the right direction. Any flexible method to bring key stakeholders together to co-sense and co-evolve a future support environment fits this kind of change effort and honors the dynamics of emergence and transformation.

Develop skills and capacities to ambidextrously manage innovation and stability in your agency and your world.

We must manage ambidextrously from a Yin/Yang perspective as this reflects the energies of the universe. For providers it means that regulatory expectations must be addressed in our daily practices. Budgets have finite qualities – revenues must meet expenses. Payroll is processed on exact dates. Repairs and maintenance are performed on routine and emergency basis to avoid decay and mechanical breakdown. There is little room for error. At the same time we are intentionally bringing forth new forms in relationship, support practice, and community engagement. This requires that we go beyond finite right/wrong, win/lose arrangements. New emerging support practices need the space for mistakes and learning. Innovation must be nurtured, not commanded. Seeking and finding the right evolutionary form challenges us to keep the game going rather than winning once and for all. If we can manage stability while simultaneously facilitating emergent practices we increase our chances of generating new responses to stuck problems while meeting current system expectations.

Evolving models of care to supports needs the nurturance found in blue spaces.

Engage as many stakeholders as possible that are impacted by the current DD system in a process of appreciative inquiry to counterbalance the negative impact of a culture of control, blame, and misinformation. It is critical that we work in the blue space across the traditional boundaries of the household, the government, non-profits, and civic organizations to see our context systemically and to foster collaborative actions. Abusive power, fundamentalism, and relentless negativity demands that a positive force of equal or greater power be invoked to encourage enlightened evolution. Engage with others in building healthy community rather than reacting emotionally to events. Assume that individuals, families, providers, and communities possess the intelligence to solve their problems collectively and create their own destiny. Invite people into a circle and build the next steps of the pathway to a desirable future today.

Above all, I invite as many of you that are willing to engage in a hero's journey to join with me in bending back the storm clouds and create ever-widening circles of blue space. I hope to see you in a community of practice or out and about in the neighborhood welcoming the gifts of diversity in our human world.

Exercises

Exercise 1:
Discovering the Resources in Our Learning Community

Objective:
  To welcome and appreciate each other and to learn about the experiences, strengths, hopes, and resources people bring to this learning/practice community.

Directions:*

1. Invite a partner to have a conversation about their interest in individualized supports and the personal resources they may contribute to a learning journey. Using the following questions spend approximately twenty minutes interviewing one partner and then switch roles to spend another twenty minutes interviewing the other partner.

   • What attracts you to the concept of person-centeredness and individualized supports? What were your initial excitements and impressions?

   • During your entire time with your agency, I'm sure you've had some ups and downs, some peaks and valleys, some highs and lows. Please reflect for a moment on a high point experience, a time when you felt most alive, most engaged, and most proud of yourself and your organization. Tell the story, what happened? What was going on?

   • What enabled your success? What was it about you (of course not discounting the contributions of others) that made your high point experience possible? What were your best qualities, skills, approaches, values, and so on that made it a great experience?

   • How could this learning/practice journey with a peer or a team support future high point experiences as you attempt to encourage innovative person-centered practices that engender individualized supports in your organization and our general community? What will make this a positive experience for you and given your personal resources how can you make that happen?

2. Each person introduces their interview partner by sharing highlights from the interview..

3. Listen for patterns and themes as others tell their stories.

   • Themes from the high point experiences

   • Skills and resources of individual members

   • Hopes about our learning/practice community

---

* If you are doing a **solo learning journey** you can use a journal to record your responses to all of the exercises.

Exercise 2:
Learning Journey Team: Deepening our Skills as Innovators of Individualized Supports

Objectives:
To determine the interest of the learning journey participants in deepening and broadening their mastery as innovators of individualized supports.

To explore the interest, energy, and capacity of the journey cohort to organize a focused learning community for the purpose of ongoing peer support, growth and learning as change agents and innovators of individualized supports.

Directions:
1. Either as a individual or as a conversation with a peer learner or learning journey team reflect upon the kinds of learning and skill development that is necessary to be an innovator, on the cutting edge of developing more individualized ways to support people. Actively inquire into other's reflections.

2. Explore these questions & complete the chart below on a flip chart:

   - What are the critical skills, knowledge, and competencies of Individualized Supports Innovators?

   - Identify other leadership development activities, people, organizations experienced by the participants that may be resource to others interested in developing individualized supports:

   - What can our learning group do to further learning and deepen knowledge, skills, and competences in the area of individualized supports?

   - What is your interest, energy, and commitment to a learning community approach? Are there any other reasons to foster ongoing connections among peers?

   - What are our first steps in organizing and implement a learning community?

   - In addition to what is in this book, what other topics and experiences could our group explore?

1. Identify skills, and knowledge that support innovative practices relative to individualized supports:	2. List potential and helpful training approaches, methods, topics that could be considered for future learning forums:	3. List other potential resources that would promote learning and understanding on how to design and implement individualized supports:	4. What roles would you be interested in playing in this learning community?

Exercise 3:
Supports Metaphor: From-To

Objectives:

To elicit metaphorical images of the present and the future potential as a way to reveal the degree of change required in your organization.

To assess your agency's readiness to generate innovation and implement individualized supports.

Directions:

1. Use the metaphor worksheet to describe your concept for innovative support. Then think of metaphors that describe current services.

2. Explore these questions:

   - How is your concept for more individualized supports different from current services: what do the contrasting metaphors say about what makes it innovative?

   - Now shift to what is expressed in the metaphor that refers to the innovation, what should you consider about organizational change, sustainability, financing, and other implementation considerations?

3. What are ways an agency could create blue space to support the development of innovative practices? Does your organization display a commitment to innovation? Where are the areas for development that will increase commitment to innovation? If you have time, generate action steps to mobilize commitment related to these indicators.

Focus of Metaphor	Metaphor Describing Your Current Services	Metaphor Describing Your Innovative & Individualized Supports Project
How the Supports are Structured & Provided.	An elevator in a department store. Select a floor for specific products & services.	A spider plant –shoots of innovative projects supported & nurtured by the main plant.
How the Team is Organized & Managed.	A classic music orchestra with a conductor. Members are consistent with defined roles.	A jazz combo –an empowered group of creative individuals with changing membership.
How a Person's Day is Experienced.	A boarding school – highly structured, programmed, & routinized.	A wilderness experience – exciting, individually defined & explored.
How Relationships between the Provider & the Person are Experienced.	Parent/child – expert, teacher, directive.	My space –network of equal relationships.

METAPHOR WORKSHEET

FOCUS OF METAPHOR	METAPHOR DESCRIBING YOUR CURRENT SERVICES	METAPHOR DESCRIBING YOUR INNOVATIVE AND INDIVIDUALIZED SUPPORTS PROJECT
HOW THE SUPPORTS ARE STRUCTURED AND PROVIDED		
HOW THE TEAM IS ORGANIZED AND MANAGED		
HOW A PERSON'S DAY IS EXPERIENCED		
HOW THE RELATIONSHIPS BETWEEN THE PROVIDER AND THE PERSON ARE EXPERIENCED		

Exercise 4:
Core Assumptions Guiding Our Practice

Objective
To surface and explore our assumptions governing our practices and context when supporting people with developmental disabilities.

Directions
1. Consider each question. Avoid politically correct answers through a process of critical assessment. You may want to think of specific people and situations as you answer each question. Identify on each answer continuum: your practice or belief with the letter *A*, your agency's practice or belief with the letter *B*, and the desired practice or belief to support individualized supports with the letter *C*.

2. Process your answers with a trusted person. Consider which side of the question aligns with individualized supports and achieving citizenship based outcomes.

---

1. What is the nature of disabilities?
People with a developmental disability are:

Abnormal/different than most people.	-------------------	The same as most people.

2. What is the nature of supports/services?
People with a developmental disability need:

Special environments to grow & learn.	-------------------	Local community & natural places to grow & learn.

3. What is our Service Orientation?
Services need to focus on:

Resolving the problems of an individual.	-------------------	Supporting people at work & in their own home.

4. What do plans focus on?
Plans must focus on:

What the person lacks in skills, appropriate behaviors, & personal resources.	-------------------	The gifts & capacities of the person.

5. Who makes the decisions?
Control for decisions should be:

In the hands of professionals with proper skills to manage complex decisions.	-------------------	With the individuals receiving services or supports.

6. How do we define quality of life? Quality of life for someone with a developmental disability is:		
Achieved with a structured & active treatment program.	--------------------	Defined by relationships, involvement in community life & roles ones assumes.
7. How do we keep people safe & avoid abuse? Individuals with a developmental disability:		
Need programs & staff to protect them from a potentially dangerous community.	--------------------	Are safest when they have family & friends.
8. How should we manage personal resources? Individuals with a developmental disability:		
Need agencies to manage their resources.	--------------------	Can manage their own resources.
9. What management style should we use to supervise staff in doing quality work?		
Productivity is promoted by a Theory X style of management.	--------------------	Productivity is promoted by a Theory Y style of management.
10. How should we govern the workplace? The nature of work relationships are:		
Hierarchical/rules based.	--------------------	Egalitarian/community oriented.
11. How do we view conflict in the workplace? The nature of conflict is:		
Destructive.	--------------------	Constructive.
12. How should we manage conflict? Conflict is best managed by:		
Competition.	--------------------	Collaboration.
13. How much personal commitment should staff have about their job? Investment of the self at work is:		
Detached.	--------------------	Involved.
14. How open should meetings be in relation to topics? The range of topics open for discussion should be:		
Many.	--------------------	Few.

15. How much learning can people do as adults?		
Adults ability to grow & learn is:		
Life long.	--------------------	Limited.

16. How much can we learn from others?		
Knowledge & expertise are:		
Shared.	--------------------	Locally focused.

17. How much role flexibility should there be in our jobs?		
Roles should be:		
Clearly designed & focused.	--------------------	Flexible & broad.

18. How much influence are we open to?		
Boundaries are:		
Firmly established & closed.	--------------------	Flexible & open.

19. How is power & influence manifested?		
Power & influence is:		
Power Over based on Position.	--------------------	Power Shared based on expertise.

Exercise 5:
Ladder of Inference

Objectives:

To raise awareness of interpretations and assumptions about people with developmental disabilities and the services agencies offer.

To better understand how our beliefs move us from observation to action and how to recognize the same thought process in others.

Directions:

1. Using a blank ladder of inference template, work through your thinking about legacy services and individualized supports.

2. Think of an important issue facing people with developmental disabilities or your agency in transforming legacy services to individualized supports.

3. Write the issue at the top of the ladder; and write three to five sentences on the Data, Interpret, Assumption and Conclusion rungs of the ladder. View an example of a completed template on page 79.

4. Divide into pairs and take turns explaining each step on you ladders. While the first member of the pair is "walking up" the ladder, the other should listen and consider the following questions:

   - Does what I'm hearing sound logical? Does it flow?

   - Is the information clear, or do I need further explanation to understand?

   - Do I understand the assumptions that are being made?

5. Using the completed template as a guide, ask your partner questions or reflect on what you have heard. For example:

   - "What events brought you to assume that individualized supports will increase the isolation of people with developmental disabilities?" (The other person replies that loneliness was discussed at change meeting.)

   - "Who was at the meeting? How long ago was it? What, if anything, has changed since then?"

   - "While I agree with your interpretation, I don't have the same assumption as you."

   - "My assumption is that people, who live in legacy homes, often live with people they don't like or relate to – hence increasing their loneliness.

   - "Because my assumption is different, my conclusion is also different. I think we need to get the conversation started at the board/administrative level.

6. After both members of the pair have explained and discussed their ladders, come back together to share general reactions, and to generate ideas about how to use the Ladder of Inference to improve communication. Keep in mind these key points:

- Practice using the ladder.
- Be patient and carefully listen to others.
- Try to correspond what you hear with each step on the ladder.
- Use this knowledge to ask better questions.

Ladder of Inference Template

I take actions based on my beliefs		
I adopt beliefs about the world		
I draw conclusions		
I make assumptions based on the meanings I added		
I add meanings (cultural and personal)		
I select "data" from what I observe		
Observable "data" and experiences		

Exercise 6:
Uncovering Our Competing Commitments*

Objective
To gain clarity and insight into the systems dynamics that thwart our goal to be innovative and create individualized supports to promote lives of distinction.

Directions
1. **Identify Our Collective Goal**: Identify a goal (e.g., individualizing supports) that meets these criteria:

   - We agree we are not doing well enough at this time.

   - We are largely responsible to work on to achieve this goal.

   - It is important that we get better at this and there are big costs if we don't.

2. **Taking a Fearless Inventory** (of behaviors contrary to the improvement goal). List concrete behaviors the system (CMS, State DD agency, providers, families, individuals, local communities) actually does or fails to do that work against the collective goal. Do not explain why various stakeholders in the system are doing these behaviors or attempt any problem solving in this step.

3. **Uncovering Your Collective Commitments**. What do I think various stakeholders should be most worried about if we tried to do the opposite of every second column entry? Turn each "worry statement" into a statement of commitment.

4. **Uncovering Our Collective "Big Assumption."** Take some individual quiet time and ask the question: *What must we assume as true if we are held back by our competing commitments?* Do not debate whether these assumptions are true or begin to problem solve instead explore the following questions:

   - Do we feel that these aspects of the mindset of various stakeholders are seriously impairing our effectiveness?

   - Do we feel like it could make a big difference if we were able to release ourselves from these group beliefs?

   - Do we owe it to ourselves to see if we can alter any of these?

1. Our Collective Goal	2. Do/Not Do Instead	3. Competing Commitments	4. Big Assumptions

---

* Adapted from Kegan and Lahey (2009)

Exercise 7:
Awakening to Your Calling*

Objectives

To identify what motivates your energy in transformational work.

To begin the process of reflective practice.

Directions

I

Reflect on the agency you work in and the people who are supported by your agency. There is something that draws you toward working with people with disabilities, particularly the people your agency. Take a minute to think about what this is.

Think about your work (including your role), the place you work and the people you come into contact with or serve. There is something that draws you toward working within that context and engaging in those activities. Take a minute to think about what this is.

I am drawn to my work with people with developmental disabilities because:

II

Thinking globally about services and supports for persons with developmental disabilities, what is the most pressing need that you think ought to be met?

How does your current role meet this larger need?

III

What is the unique personal significance you feel that you make in relationship to the needs you described above? This is different from the skills that you bring to the job. This is about your genuine talent and your authentic contribution that makes you deeply qualified for the work that needs to be done.

---

* Carol Blessing designed the first version of this exercise.

My genuine talents and authentic contribution to the work of supporting persons with developmental disabilities is/are:

IV

Most of us who supervise, lead teams or teach can acknowledge that we are loosely connected to a general idea about why we do the work we do. Yet often times when we become more specific, as to why and how to do our work, we find that our responses become much more personally defined and individualized. Place an "x" on the line below to show to what degree that you feel that all of the members of your team and/or your agency share a common purpose for the work and achieving high performance and desired results.

Large Degree   *Some Degree*   *No Degree*

V

A strong component for successful leadership and education is to become purposefully aware of the dynamics that are pushing team members out of alignment with one another. Think about the past six months in your work. Undoubtedly you have been involved in, or witness to, times of stress and conflict between departments and/or individuals. Very likely these situations reflected same-old-same-old scenarios (same stuff/different day), and when all was said and done, you were left feeling discouraged, frustrated or angry at the way the issue was resolved or handled.

What do you think creates the greatest challenge for people where you work, to work as individual and collective members of a team, to be committed toward resolving issues in the context of a shared purpose? As you think about your answers, try to avoid the temptation to make broad and sweeping general statements. Be specific about the actual experiences that you have on a regular basis.

Organizational Challenge(s) – structures and processes: are there things in the day-to-day operation where you work or in the structure of how services or supports are delivered that contribute to making the work harder than it needs to be?

Relationship Challenge(s) – interpersonal dynamics: are there patterns of behavior and interactions that people have come to anticipate, accept and/or to reinforce that actually work at cross-purposes? Think about your ability to address issues in the open, to work through conflict and to respond to one another from a position of appreciation and respect.

Personal Challenge(s) – Individual skills and abilities: are there expectations in your work environment that require specific skill sets that are not readily present or available? Are you able to bring out your personal best on a regular basis at work?

VI

Principles are the internal processes that guide our behavior on a regular basis. They establish the criteria by which we set our standards and the lens through which we view the world. In a way, they are the basis for sentences that include words like "should" and "ought" in them.

Use the key below to put the letter that best represents the frequency in which you believe that each of the following principles are operating in your work and in your respective teams.

A=Always   S=Sometimes   R=Rarely   G=Generally   N=Never

_____Fairness   _____Integrity   _____Kindness   _____Respect

_____Service   _____Contribution   _____Appreciation

_____Trustworthiness   _____Other (please identify) _____

Team Building Activity:
1. Complete this activity in advance of a team development session. You will be sharing your response with your team.
2. We learn best when we teach others. Learning is internalized when we live it.

   Imagine for a moment that you are the Enlightened One from whom people will travel great distances to seek your counsel and wisdom. Each day, you entertain one question that the multitudes bring to you. A Truth-Seeker will climb the mountain to sit with you to ask the daily question and to acquire important knowledge that they will take back down the mountain with them. They will share this knowledge with members in their communities and your word will spread in meaningful ways to the good of all humankind.

   Today, the truth seekers are asking you to respond to this question:

Out of all of the principles listed above, which is the one principle that you think that, if intentionally practiced with more regularity in your work place or your team that would make a world of positive difference.

What is the principle that you recommend?

Why did you elect this principle?

What is the message about this principle that you would have the Truth-Seeker carry back down the mountain to spread?

Exercise 8:

Finding Your Voice: Becoming the Change You Seek[*]

Objectives

To identify the "whole person" resources that you bring to the innovation journey.

To locate your "personal voice" that guides and centers you as you function as a resource for yourself and others during the innovation and change process.

Directions

1. Using flip chart paper, individually complete your whole person profile using the designated categories.

2. Determine your unique "voice" or contributions to your team, your organization's mission, and to the innovative project on individualized services you are interested in developing.

3. Share the results from your individual work with a mentor or fellow traveler on the transformation journey.

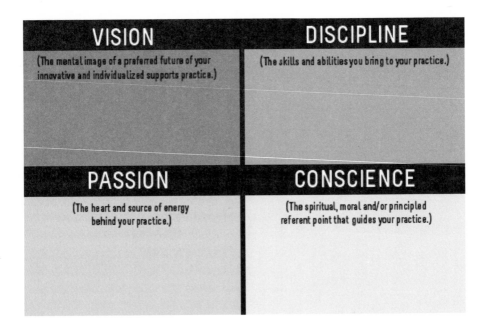

VISION	DISCIPLINE
(The mental image of a preferred future of your innovative and individualized supports practice.)	(The skills and abilities you bring to your practice.)
PASSION	**CONSCIENCE**
(The heart and source of energy behind your practice.)	(The spiritual, moral and/or principled referent point that guides your practice.)

---

[*] Adapted from Steven Covey (2004).

Exercise 9:
Levels of Individual-Support Provider Relationship

Objectives

To locate the current relational orientation between an individual and a provider.

To identify a desired relational form between an individual and a provider of supports.

Directions

On each line, put an "N" and an "F" to show about how much of your work happens at each level Now and how much of your work you want to happen at this level in the Future (don't worry about how the change could happen, just show where you would like to be).

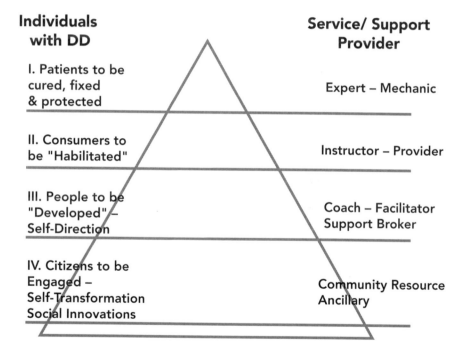

Individuals with DD	Service/ Support Provider
I. Patients to be cured, fixed & protected	Expert – Mechanic
II. Consumers to be "Habilitated"	Instructor – Provider
III. People to be "Developed" – Self-Direction	Coach – Facilitator Support Broker
IV. Citizens to be Engaged – Self-Transformation Social Innovations	Community Resource Ancillary

Exercise 10:
How Individualized is the Support or Service?

Objective
To determine if your agency's supports or services are individualized or innovative.

Directions

I

Using this grid, rate your agency or a specific service in your agency against the critical elements of individualization.

Degree of Individualization

Critical Elements	Low (checks in this column are weighted as a one)	Medium (checks in this column are weighted as a two)	High (checks in this column are weighted as a three)
Choice			
Decision Making			
Personal Space			
Social Integration			
Total all three columns for your score			

Scores of 8 and above qualify as a potential innovation in individualized supports.

II

Now test your supports and services for their degree and level of individualized design.

Identify where in your organization are examples of level one, two or three individualization.

Justify your selection by testing it against the following questions:

- Identify the support and/or service and its level on the Individualized Supports Grid.
- Were the supports uniquely created around each individual's distinct vision for their life (rather than a funding stream)?
- Did you use individual planning processes that primarily included each focus person and the people who are important to him/her?
- Did the individual planning processes promote shared decision making with each person and their family where appropriate)? How so?
- Are the supports unique (not grouped or arranged with others flexible, portable) for each individual?

- Are the supports implemented within a continuing partnership arrangement with the individual and the family(where appropriate)?

- Are the person specific supports arranged in such as way as to assist a person achieve a chosen valued outcome in work, relationships, health and home?

- What valued roles in home, leisure, work and civic life will the individually designed supports intentionally help realize for each participant in this project?

III

Answer these questions in reference to the degree to which your organization promotes service and support innovation:

- Have you introduced a new service or support that may assist an individual or family achieve a valued outcome or life of distinction?

- Does your project decouple individuals being supported in a group arrangement, hence moving away from traditionally structured services?

- Does your project require that your agency (or part of it) have to significantly alter service structures, practices, and/or processes?

- Does your project require changes in how the support is financed?

- Does your project significantly change the relationship between the provider and person supported to one of "power with" vs. "power over"?

- Do new individualized supports significantly broaden the commitments of support and relationship beyond the agency to the community?

- Do new supports require personal change and the challenging of core beliefs of the innovators and implementers?

Step 4:

Assess the gap between your present supports and services and the capacity to support lives of distinction with innovative individualized support designs. This process will provide insight into the degree your organization may have to commit to an adaptive learning journey.

Exercise 11:
Person-Centered Friendly Organization Survey

Part 1: The Organization

1. These questions relate to your understanding of your organization's vision.						
To what extent… (mark one on each line)	Not at All	Not Much	Some-what	Much	Very Much	Don't Know
Does the vision of your organization reflect an individualized, person-centered support orientation?						
Is the vision shared at all levels in the organization?						
Is the vision supported by key stakeholder (family, individuals, local government, other providers)?						
Is your organization's strategy for reaching the vision clear to you?						

2. These questions relate to the core services provided by this organization to persons with intellectual & developmental disabilities.						
To what extent… (mark one on each line)	Not at All	Not Much	Some-what	Much	Very Much	Don't Know
Are supports & services based on a holistic view of the persons including their unique gifts, capacities, interests, preferences & support needs?						
Do individuals outcomes & goals reflect increased self-direction, valued roles in jobs, desired home life & lifestyle, & the experience of citizenship contribution & close personal relationships?						
Does the individual guide the planning process, experience authentic choices, & is in a partnership with their support worker?						
Are the resources flexible enough to be used for unique solutions for each individual as opposed to being designed for a group?						

3. The following questions relate to this organization's structures, processes, policies, & practices.						
To what extent… (mark one on each line)	Not at All	Not Much	Some-what	Much	Very Much	Don't Know
Do policies & procedures support person-centered practices?						

Does the design of my job allow me to be flexible enough to do person-centered work?						
Are decisions made in a participatory fashion?						
Are communication practices open, timely, & effective?						

4. The following questions relate to this organization's culture.

To what extent... (mark one on each line)	Not at All	Not Much	Some-what	Much	Very Much	Don't Know
Do your peers & employees hold themselves accountable to individualized, person-centered quality services & outcomes?						
Are disagreements or conflicts with others seen as opportunities to learn & solve problems?						
Are new ideas & creative solutions supported by others?						
Are people of all races, gender, disability & cultural backgrounds included & productive in the workplace?						

5. The following questions relate to management practices in your organization.

To what extent (mark one on each line)...	Not at All	Not Much	Some-what	Much	Very Much	Don't Know
Does management encourage an environment of openness & trust?						
Does management prioritize, measure & reward job performance based on person-centered, individualized outcomes?						
Does management encourage, accept & implement new ideas & approaches?						
Do managers assume a coaching role to help employees understand job expectations, develop skills, & get the resources they need to do their job effectively?						

Part 2: Individual Supports

The indicators of principles are based on six valued outcomes (i.e., safety, community participation, choice, respect, competence, and relationships) that a person-centered friendly agency is working to achieve with the people we support. The survey is designed to discover the degree to which your agency aligns with person-centered values and supports.

Please read each question and place a check mark in the box that best represents your perspective. Please think in the aggregate, i.e., a response which will be true for most people served by your agency.

Integrated Planning (Person Centered)	Always	Usually	Some-times	Seldom	Never
The integrated support plan is based on a person's interests, preferences, strengths & capabilities. The daily activities/supports lead logically to valued outcomes.					
Services & supports are designed for each individual.					
Services & supports are individualized & directly relate to valued outcomes.					
The person(s) or those who best know them are selecting the overarching goals.					
The person(s) or those who best know them participate in meetings where important plans/decisions are made.					
Progress towards goals & valued outcomes are measured objectively & monitored on regular or as needed basis.					
The person's planning team includes family & friends, independent advocates or staff who care about the person.					
The full range of quality of life issues associated with major life style decisions are discussed at each person's meeting.					
Most individuals have frequent opportunities to express (dis)satisfaction with their home, work, daily routines, & relationships.					
Problematic aspects of a person's lifestyle are researched, & where possible positive changes are made.					
Persons or those who know them best make decisions about major & minor uses of resources.					

Funding has been tailored to support an individualized service plan for most persons.					
Attendance at planning meetings is fairly stable.					
Planning meetings are well facilitated & promote collaboration among members.					
Choice	Always	Usually	Some-times	Seldom	Never
Most people supported by your agency are helped to understand the alternatives before making choices in areas in which they are not experienced.					
Important choices about home décor, space, location are made by the person to the greatest extent possible.					
Most people your agency supports, or people who know them best, select desired personal goals & outcomes to pursue.					
Important choices about work desires, preferences, & schedule are made by the people your agency supports to the greatest extent possible.					
Staff assist individuals in expressing preferences & choice as they go about their everyday routines.					
Decisions about a person's daily free time are made by the individual or those who know him/her best.					
Most people your agency supports have appropriate control of their own resources.					
Most people your agency supports have opportunities to spend their own money.					
Most people your agency supports make choices about when & what to eat.					
Most people your agency supports make decisions about their clothing, what to wear every day, when to bath & shower.					
Most people your agency supports decide when to go bed, when to get up, & when to take naps.					
Most persons can engage in minor vices, such smoking, drinking, over-eating, drinking coffee, reading sexually explicit magazines.					

Respect	Always	Usually	Some-times	Seldom	Never
Most people supported by your agency live & work in environments & engage in activities that minimize the potential for stigmatizing &/or devaluing them.					
Most people supported by your agency have appearances that promote dignity & respect.					
Most people your agency supports can interact in ways in public that promotes being accepted by others in the community.					
Staff always communicate with people your agency supports in a manner that promotes respect & a positive social image.					
Most people your agency supports assume a valued role that adds value & is an important part of a product, service, or has other benefits to society.					
Staff support people in ways that promote enhanced images & roles & avoid negative images.					

Community Presence & Participation	Always	Usually	Some-times	Seldom	Never
Family members, neighbors, friend, co-workers or other natural supports are usually included in a person's social activities & relationships.					
Most people your agency supports make use of typical community resources for health care, recreation, shopping, banking, meals, & transportation.					
Most people your agency supports visit a variety of community locations in living, working, recreating, & getting support.					
Most persons your agency supports spend their time in settings where most people do not have developmental disabilities.					
Most people who your agency supports live in a typical community setting.					
Most people your agency supports assume active & meaningful roles in community clubs, churches, or other organized groups.					

Relationships	Always	Usually	Some-times	Seldom	Never
Most people your agency supports have regularly recurring relationships with people from the community who do not have disabilities.					
Generally speaking, most people your agency supports enjoy & get along with the people they live with.					
Generally speaking, most people your agency supports get along well with staff.					
Generally speaking most people your agency support are personally close with at least one other person.					
Most people supported by your agency have an opportunity to spend quality time with friends & family.					
Most persons are supported by your agency in pursuing relationships in which they are interested.					

Enhancing Competence	Always	Usually	Some-times	Seldom	Never
Most persons are able to achieve the personal goals they set out for themselves.					
Most persons supported by your agency are employed in competitive, supported &/ or voluntary jobs.					
Most persons are given the opportunity to be promoted to job duties or activities of greater complexity or pay.					
During the work or day activity, most persons do things that increase their skills & competencies that will help them achieve other valued outcomes.					
Most persons are learning to exert greater control & influence over the circumstances in their life that will help them achieve valued outcomes.					

Safety	Always	Usually	Some-times	Seldom	Never
Most individuals have people in their lives that love them & care about their welfare.					
Most people your agency supports live in settings that are nurturing not abusive.					
Most people who are socially or physical vulnerable are provided the necessary sup-ports from your agency to protect them from unnecessary harm & risk.					
Most people your agency supports work in settings that are physically safe.					
Most people socially frequent places that are safe or free from potential harm & exploitation.					
Most people your agency supports receive appropriate medical &/or clinical sup-ports.					
Most people your agency supports are protected from situations that are stigma-tizing.					

Exercise 12:
Learning Journey Observational Guide

Objectives

Provide perspective on how individualized supports can be negotiated, designed and implemented.

Spark creative thinking on how an organization (yours) might approach an innovative practice,

Get a sense of the practical considerations in approaching the development of individualized supports.

Compare and contrast how various organizations design and implement individualized supports.

Understand the management and leadership orientations that foster innovation and individualized supports.

Learn how your state DD Agency funding supports or inhibits individualized approaches.

Directions

Going on a site visit is reflective practice in action. The learning cycle is a helpful tool for you and your team to apply as you engage in site visits.

The worksheet on the next page presents questions to consider when you conduct a site visit.

IMPRESSIONS OF THE HOST ORGANIZATION	
How different or alike is the host organization from yours?	
What surprised you during your visit to the host organization?	
What creative thoughts were sparked by your visit to the host organization?	
How does the visit to the host organization impact upon your prototype concept? Does it change it, reinforce it?	
CULTURE, VALUES, LEADERSHIP	
What kind of culture & leadership does the host organization have? How did this help or hinder innovative practice?	
What are the host organization's views & values about individuals with disabilities?	
How did the host organization integrate individualized supports into the rest of the organization?	
INVOLVEMENT/ENGAGEMENT	
How are families & individuals with disabilities involved in the creation & implementation of innovative practices around individualized supports?	
How are direct care professionals involved in the design & implementation of individualized supports?	
How did the organization engage its key stakeholders as allies in the provision of individualized supports?	

KNOWLEDGE/ STRUCTURE	
What do I/We need/want to know about innovation & individualized supports?	
How did the host organization prepare itself for innovative practice?	
What kind of organizational structure does the host organization have? How does it help or hinder innovative practice?	
What kind of challenges has the organization faced (& overcome) in the creation of individualized supports?	
What strategies did the host organization use to build human resource capacity for the provision of individualized supports?	

Exercise 13:
Letting Go and Dancing with Our Dragons[*]

Objective

To move into a place where new perspectives and potentials come into view by letting go of typical ways of interpreting, responding, and placing ourselves in our everyday world.

To identify the consuming fears (change dragons) which block our capacity to create and innovate new sustainable responses.

To create a safe space through the use of an appreciative frame of reference. The assumption behind this exercise is that by acknowledging our change dragons and appreciating the human experience of the change process, we can "dance with our dragons" and create the conditions for social innovation.

Directions

I. Individual Work (20 minutes)

1. Read this poem.

Letting Go
(Author unknown)

To "let go" does not mean to stop caring,
it means I can't do it for someone else.

To "let go" is not to cut myself off,
it's the realization I can't control another.

To "let go" is not to enable,
but to allow learning from natural consequences.

To "let go" is to admit powerlessness,
which means the outcome is not in my hands.

To "let go" is not to try to change or blame another,
it's to make the most of myself.

To "let go" is not to care for,
but to care about.

---

[*] Thanks to Sandy Van Eck and Chris Saj for the original design of this exercise.

To "let go" is not to fix,
but to be supportive.

To "let go" is not to judge,
but to allow another to be a human being.

To "let go" is not to be in the middle arranging the outcomes,
but to allow others to affect their own destinies.

To "let go" is not to be protective,
it's to permit another to face reality.

To "let go" is not to deny,
but to accept.

To "let go" it not to nag, scold or argue,
but instead to search out my own shortcomings, and correct them.

To "let go" is not to adjust everything to my desires
but to take each day as it comes,
and cherish myself in it.

To "let go" is not to criticize and regulate anybody
but to try to become what I dream I can be.

To "let go" is not to regret the past,
but to grow and live for the future.

To "let go" is to fear less,
and love more

2. Reorder the poem's sentences and paragraphs to reflect your experience working with individuals with a disability.

3. Reflect on these questions:

   - When have you had difficulty letting go of routine ways of responding to people, typical roles you assume, or common ways of viewing the world when new and creative responses were required? In what circumstances? What was the impact on the person with a disability?

   - If you let go of your typical roles, responses and perspectives, how would it change the conversation, the relationships you have with individuals and/or the kind of actions you take? What would it look like?

   4. Record this in your journal.

II. Group Work (20-30 minutes)

4. Process "letting go" experiences with your learning team (if it is just you – use your journal to process your experiences)

5. Each individual learner shares a story of "letting go" of traditional roles, responses and perspectives related to supporting a person with a disability. Included in the individual stories are illustrations of how letting go effected change and innovation related to how a person was supported and the kind of personal outcomes that may have resulted.

6. As peer learners describe their experiences, common themes should be noted.

III. Individual Work (20 minutes)

7. Take a twenty-minute walk to reflect upon your consuming fears (change dragons) in relationship to "letting go" of assumptions, roles, and relationships connected with a legacy service orientation.

8. After returning from your walk, you (and your peer learners) should write down their fears/change dragons in a locked box (without identifying yourself on the paper). By locking away fears and assumptions you are preparing for the innovation learning journey.

Group Work (20-30 minutes)

9. Open the locked box at a future date. If in a learning team, each peer learner will reach in the box and take a piece of paper with a written statement of fear and share that it says with one another peer. Remember, no one's individual fears will be identified.

10. Peer learners will identify the types of fears/change dragons emerging from the locked box to the whole learning team.

Exercise 14:
Learning Journal:
Questions for the Reflective Practitioner:

The Learning Journal assists you in this developmental journey by offering a set of questions for you to consider and reflect upon:

- At what developmental level are you starting this journey?
- Does a practical individualized supports project you have initially put forth to pursue in the learning journey challenge the operating practices of your agency, push the envelope, entail change in practice, leadership mindset, service orientation, customer/provider roles, and/or constitute risk for you and your agency?
- What are the key ideas and motivators, personally and organizationally, that shape your approach to this learning journey?
- What kinds of changes do you see yourself going through as you participate in a learning journey?
- How are you preparing yourself for new innovative practices? Designing, promoting and implementing innovations in organizations requires vision, personal persistence/resilience, interpersonal and political skill, the ability to tolerate complex/contradictory tensions and work within ambiguous work situations. What do you think? Does this excite or depress you (or both)?
- Innovation and Change possess challenges for any organization, what are the key challenges for your agency?
- Do you anticipate resistance to any proposed innovation projects by some groups or individuals in your organization? How do you plan to work with this?
- Reflect on the key assumptions about change in your organization.
- Reflect on the key assumptions about change in your own practice (or role) and mind set about your work.
- How does this project reflect the vision you have for individuals with disabilities and the future service orientation of your organization and your practice?
- Have you given any thought to how an innovative support will be integrated into your agency?
- What strategies will you use to involve others and spread the innovation?
- How will the benefits of change be shared with the larger community (inside and outside your organization)?
- Are you interested, excited and committed in participating in a mutual learning community? A community that gives to you as much as you contribute to it.
- Other learning questions you would find valuable in reflecting upon in this journey:

Glossary

Appreciation: an acute awareness of the positive essence of people and community and the inherent value of diversity in any system. This awareness stems from an openness to hear, feel, and experience other points of view. Appreciation is enacted through an empathetic orientation that seeks to deeply understand a person, a context and the connections of a situation or a system, large or small. It is practically carried out through a process of inquiry and advocacy.

Appreciative Culture: the culture of an organization that acts on the assumption that the capacities of people and the diversity of its stakeholders are keys to its effectiveness and long-term sustainability. Appreciative culture, through its leaders, structures, processes, and practices builds on the strengths of the organization and its people by challenging, nurturing, and providing resources to enact a positive, productive and sustainable workplace.

Appreciative Inquiry (AI): an organization development method that works to build on what is strong and positive in an organization. The method can be described as relentlessly curious and inquisitive about the interests, purpose, capacities, and desires of an organization's membership to create a future of its own choosing. AI has been used in many ways as a method to built culture, set future directions, and increase team effectiveness. In its inquiry summit form AI cycles through four days of discovering an organization's positive core, dreaming (envisioning) an organizations greatest future contribution, designing a strategy to build on its positive core and realize its future vision and create an action plan to move towards its destiny. http://appreciativeinquiry.case.edu/

Capitation Payments: refers to a payment arrangement for health care providers (hospitals, nursing homes, doctors). Typically the payment is determined by averaging the health care costs of a certain segment of the population and paid out to service providers or a managed care company on a per month per patient fee structure.

Chaordic Organization: refers to a system that has the features of both chaos and order as critical elements in designing organizations. http://www.chaordic.org/

Circle of Support: Beth Mount defines Circles of Support as a group of "people who care about change happening for the focus person and choose to give their time and resources to working for change. They see themselves as an action oriented group that exists with and for the person, commit themselves to working alongside the focus person and meeting from time to time for as long as it takes to assure that the person has a secure and interesting community life." (Mount, 2002)

Community of Practice: a group of people who share a common interest, practice or domain who voluntarily meet and have a goal of sharing knowledge, information, and/or experiences to improve a situation and/or their practice or technical understanding of a discipline.

Day Treatment: an original legacy group-based program funded by Medicaid, clinically oriented and usually implemented in class room settings focused on activities of daily living, crafts, and therapeutic interventions such as physical, occupational, and speech therapies.

Deinstitutionalization: the process of releasing "patients" to the community or moving the supports for people with disabilities from hospitals and other large service settings (the institution) to small group homes and programs in the community.

Developmental Center: large institutions for persons with developmental disabilities.

Dialogic Processes: processes that encourage critical thinking, an understanding of differences among people, and the deep exploration of meaning and underlying assumptions and values that operate in relationships and in organizations.

Fee for Service: a payment arrangement that is based on reimbursing each service after it is delivered.

Fiscal Intermediary: is an entity that performs administrative functions such as financial and human resource management services for an individual with DD that directs their own budget and services.

Future Search: is a three day large group meeting that addresses complex social issues with a focus on finding common ground and developing action plans based on consensus. http://www.futuresearch.net/

Generative (Leadership): the term "generative" is defined as the ability to give birth to new ideas and actions, bring good things into being or to evoke. Generative leaders, therefore, are leaders that create organizational contexts for something new, powerful and innovative to be brought forth to enact a more effective and sustainable workplace and world.

Gestalt Therapy: a method of psychotherapy based on Gestalt psychology, which looks at the human mind and behavior in wholes rather than breaking it into parts. Heavily based in humanism, Gestalt therapy was concerned with the perceptual process and how people established and maintained functional boundaries with themselves and others.

Individual Residential Alternative (IRA): is a type of community residence that provides room, board and (theoretically) individualized service options for individuals with DD, typically in groups of 4-8.

Intermediate Care Facility (ICF-MR): A health care facility for individuals who are disabled, elderly, or non-acutely ill, usually providing less intensive care than that offered at a hospital or skilled nursing home. ICF-MR, a Medicaid funded program, was applied to institutions (developmental centers) and group homes during the late 1970's through today.

Inquiry and Advocacy: are a set of personal skills and an interpersonal approach to understand a person, a proposal, a human and organizational dynamic, or a situation. Inquiry is a process that is enacted by way of openness and curiosity of one person to explore data, perception, assumptions, and conclusions that lead to a proposal for action or a behavior of another person. Advocacy is clearly articulating in a transparent fashion all the prior ingredients mentioned for inquiry to give people an understanding of where one's proposal or behavior is coming from. Inquiry and advocacy work more effectively in a dialogic process in which judgment and evaluation are suspended in favor of developing understanding and clarity.

Legacy Services: services designed and implemented in 1970s for persons with developmental disabilities as an alternative to large institutions, notably developmental centers. Group homes, sheltered workshops, day treatment programs and group-based day habilitation are examples of legacy services.

Medicaid: a United States jointly funded (Federal/State) health-financing program for people with low incomes and persons with disabilities.

NYSACRA (New York State Association of Community and Residential Agencies): is a trade association for dues paying DD providers in New York State.

Open Space Technology: is a large group planning meeting that has the distinction of having no agenda other than the theme of the event. The assumption is that what is truly important to the participants will drive the meeting, a pure approach to social constructivism. http://www.openspaceworld.org/

Organization Development (OD): is a professional field of social action and an area of scientific inquiry. The OD practice of organizational change, improvement, and intervention is largely based on humanistic philosophy, behavioral science, and social construction theory and methodology. The key purpose of OD is to produce positive, productive, effective, and ultimately sustainable workplaces. Over the years many methods and disciplines have fallen under the umbrella of OD such as organizational diagnosis and feedback, leading and managing change, leadership development, interpersonal and group process consultation, team building, conflict resolution, work and job design, human resource management, and more recently organizational learning and transformation, appreciative inquiry, and many of the large group interventions (Future Search, Open-Space Technology and World Café).

Paid Neighbors: an alternative way to unobtrusively support a person with a developmental disability for a minimal amount time (typically 10 hours or less per week). The paid neighbor lives near the person and is available to support the individual socially and for emergencies. Most of the time, this form of support is supplement to paid staff in a support arrangement.

Rational Management: is an important, but single frame approach that assumes that organizations exist primarily to accomplish established goals. The emphasis is on appropriately designing organizational structures with the right balance of differentiation, integration, coordination, (de)centralization, and control of the work. It further assumes that the future can be determined and that with rational analysis and goal planning, this future state can be achieved. Absent from the rational management frame is the human element (people and their drives), politics, and the meaning of symbolic events, leadership actions and culture on an organizational and system.

Reflective Practitioner: Donald Schon defines the reflective practitioner as having: "the capacity to reflect on action so as to engage in a process of continuous learning." This capacity is enhanced by critical thinking, a double and triple loop learning process, learning and application of theory, and skills of inquiry and advocacy – all in service of professional and personal development and effectiveness.

Single, Double, and Triple Loop Learning: Single loop learning is concerned correcting variances to a pre-determined goal or standard. Double-loop learning relates to trying another way at solving a problem. Triple loop learning is about surfacing, reflecting upon and transforming our functional assumptions, beliefs, thinking process, and approaches to solve a problem. Single loop learning addresses skill development for first order change (correcting a problem), double loop learning reframes a problem for second order change (finding creative solutions), and triple loop learning alters our worldview leading to transformational change.

Shared Living: an alternative support arrangement in which a person with a development disability chooses to share their life with another person (typically a person or family without disabilities) in a home either owned or leased by the person with DD or co-owned/co-leased by all the people residing in the home. The person without a disability is commonly referred to a "shared living provider" and has roles and responsibilities that have deeper connections and share power with the person with DD.

Socio-Technical Design: an OD method that considers the social as well as the technical aspects of tasks in designing work and jobs.

Social Constructivism: is a theory and philosophy based on the assumption that reality and truth is created by people in collaboration. Groups create meaning and knowledge that applies to their everyday world. We literally construct our world through conversation and interaction.

Social Justice: is exercised within a society when the principle of equality and a fair distribution of all resources is present in communities and systems throughout a nation. It inherently recognizes the rights of all people and the dignity of every human being.

Total Quality Management: is an integrative philosophy and set of tools and methods of management for continuously improving the quality of products and processes originally developed by W. Edwards Demming.

Willowbrook Developmental Center: located on Staten Island in New York City, was at one time the largest institution in the US for people with DD. Closed as a result of a consent degree that settled a lawsuit responding to widespread neglect and abuse at the center.

World Café: a large group session designed to encourage open dialogue among key stakeholders regarding topics of interest and concern to the target group. http://www.theworldcafe.com/

Notes

1. Bill Moyers interviewed the philosopher Philip Hallie on the PBS Special "Facing Evil" in 1988.

2. An interview with Ricard Matthieu, a Buddhist Monk "A Patch of Blue Sky" by David Ulrich in Collective Intelligence, 2006

3. Albert Einstein and Leopold Infeld, 1938

4. Blatt and Kaplan 1974.

5. Rivera, G. 1972.

6. I owe my understanding of the concept of good form to Joseph C. Zinker, 1998

7. Hallie 1988

8. Scharmer 2007.

9. Meissner 2011.

10. Walker, P. 2011.

11. Schein, 1992 p. 12

12. See Castellani, 2005.

13. I obtained my Ph.D. from what was then called the Institute for Experimenting Colleges and Universities (now The Union Institute) which concept and structure was based on one of its founder's book: Roy Fairfield's *Person-Centered Graduate Education*. 1977.

14. Scharmer, 2007.

15. SRV, social role valorization, an analysis of human relationships and human services, formulated in 1983 by Wolf Wolfensberger and delivered in a training format to employees of DD agencies throughout the world.

16. Scharmer 2007

17. Kegan, 2009

18. Thanks to George Garin for Brian's story.

19. Mary (1998) discusses the evolution of service delivery for people with developmental disabilities from the medical model to the developmental model to the current support model. She states that the current service delivery paradigm

has changed the conceptualization of consumers, service intent, and the role of professionals.

20. Hugh Lafave, former progressive director of Eleanor Roosevelt Developmental Services in Schenectady, New York. Gunner Dybwad prominent advocate for people with developmental disabilities. Wolf Wolfensberger a university professor who influenced disability policy and practice with his development of Social Role Valorisation (SRV).

21. Conditions grouped under the label "developmental disability" and expanded to include certain other neurological conditions in 1970 federal legislation. Construction Amendments of 1970 (P.L. 91-517). Renamed as the Developmental Disabilities Assistance Act.

22. Wheatley 2012, p. 212

23. Mount, 2007

24. Kuhn, 1996. The contemporary meaning of a paradigm, although not originally meant to describe social phenomenon, clarifies what is going on in the evolution of DD service. Paradigm shift, a term coined by Thomas Kuhn 28 (1996), describes a prevailing way society goes about organizing its beliefs and assumptions to make sense out of reality.

25. Thanks to Julia Kelly for Loree's story

26. Campbell, 1996

27. Wheatley, 2009

28. Block, 200325

29. Emery and Trist (1973) came up with the original design for large group future search conferences. Others that contributed to the development of this method were Eva Schindler-Rainman and Ronald Lippitt (1980) – see Building the Collaborative Community, Mobilizing Citizens for Action. In the 1990s, Weisbord and Janoff brought the method into the mainstream of planning practices.

30. From John O'Brien & Carol Blessing, 2011, used with permission

31. http://www.famous-quotes.cc/authors/fritz-perls

32. Kagan and Lahey 2009

33. Viesturs, 2009 It must be obvious that hiking and mountains are my passion.

34. Kendrick (212) explores the importance on understanding the kind of agency transformation being sought when individualizing supports in legacy settings.

35. Ackerman-Anderson, 1986

36. Waivers are vehicles states can use to test new or existing ways to deliver and pay for health care services in Medicaid and the Children's Health Insurance Program (CHIP.)

37. Scharmer, 2007

38. Waivers are vehicles states can use to test new or existing ways to deliver and pay for health care services in Medicaid and the Children's Health Insurance Program (CHIP.)

39. Arygis (1995) and Senge (1990) influence much of our interpersonal, team and agency development.

40. Kagan and Lahey, 2009

41. Senge, 1990

42. Tim Merry is a social entrepreneur, slam poet and experienced facilitator.

43. Cheuna-Judge's 2001 article on The Self as an Instrument is a great resource in developing effectiveness as a leader and OD Professional.

44. Campbell, 1968

45. Modified from Jennifer Garvey Berger (2006) on Adult Forms of Understanding

46. Communities of Practice (Wenger, 2002) and Appreciative Inquiry (Cooperider, 2000) are methods that represent a new generation of organization development practice. These methods are based on a constructivist belief that humans create their own reality through conversation and ongoing interaction.

47. My thinking in the area of leadership development has been informed by Torbert and Cook-Greuter, 2005 and Robert Kegan's theory of adult development, 1982.

48. http://www.likeablequotes.com/rapport-quotes-1360.html

49. Rogers (1961)

50. These paragraphs are informed by Peter Senge, 2010 and Chris Arygis, 1974.

51. These paragraphs are informed by the Gestalt Cycle of Experience, E.C. Nevis, 1987.

52. Miles Davis Interview, 1988. http://www.youtube.com/watch?v=Upig0UoU27U)

53. Adapted from: Kaeufer, K., Scharmer, O.C., and Verteegen, U. (2003). Breathing Life into a Dying System: Recreating Health Care from Within. *Reflections 5*, 3.

54. http://www.goodreads.com/quotes/876-to-be-yourself-in-a-world-that-is-constantly-trying

55. SANYS, 2007. Information about Self Advocacy Association of New York State can be found at http://sanys.org/

56. Putnam, 2000

57. Resources from Marc Gold and his associates can be found at http://www.marc-gold.com/

58. March, 2011

59. Schein 1992 Pg. 363

60. Statement from the Board of the Change Agent Series for Groups and Organizations, 2001 from Cummings and Worley, 2005

61. Further resources on the field of organization development can be found in the Adison-Wesley Series on organization development and Jossey-Bass/Pfeiffer's *The Practicing Organization Development Series.*

62. For more information about these large group interventions: Brown, J.B. and Isaacs, D. *The World Café*; Cooperrider, D. L., Whitney, D., & Stavros, J. M.. *Appreciative Inquiry Handbook;* Owen, H., *Open Space Handbook.*

63. Schein, 1992, page 363

64. I learned about "deep dives" from Scharmer, 2007.

65. Ambidextrous, as it is applied to the quality of an organization and its leadership was first applied by Tushman, 2009. Quinn and Cameron's Competing Values Framework (1999), Deal and Bolman's Four Frame Model (2008), and ultimately Tushman and O'Reilly's (1997) *Winning Through Innovation.*

66. See James Carse, 1987 for a wonderful explanation of this quality of seeing and acting.

67. Using metaphors to inspire new ways to design organization was informed by Gareth Morgan, 1993.

68. Emerson, Famous Quotes

69. Block, 2008

70. A term coined by Beth Mount and applied in the NYSACRA Learning Institute on Innovations of Individualized Supports.

71. NESTA, 2010

72. Senge, 2010, referencing Humberto Maturana, page 335

73. Scharmer, 2007

74. Dancing with Dragons metaphor was inspired by Joseph Campbell, 1988 and Rebecca Chan Allen, 2002.

75. Hock, 1999

76. Joseph Campbell, The Power of the Myth 1988

77. Michael Kendrick, 2000

References

Berger, J.G. (2006). Adult Development Theory and Executive Coaching Practice. In Stober, D.R. and Grant, A. M. *Evidence Based Coaching Handbook*. Hoboken, NJ: Wiley Publishers. Pp. 77-102.

Block, P. (2003). *The Answer to How is Yes: Acting on What Matters*. San Francisco, CA: Berrett-Koehler Publishers.

Block, P. (2008). *Community: The Structure of Belonging*. San Francisco, CA: Berrett-Koehler Publishers.

Brown, J and Isaacs, D. (2005). *The World Café, Shaping Our Futures Through Conversations that Matter*. San Francisco CA. Berrett-Koehler.

Blatt, B and Kaplan, F. (1974). *Christmas in Purgatory: A Photographic Essay on Mental Retardation*. Syracuse NY: Human Policy Press.

Campbell, J. (1968). *The Hero with a Thousand Faces*. Princeton NJ: Princeton Press.

Campbell, J. with Moyers, B. (1988). *The Power of Myth*. New York: Doubleday.

Campbell, J. (1991). The Joseph Campbell Companion. New York: Harper Collins Publishers.

Carse, J. (1986). *Finite and Infinite Games*. New York: Free Press.

Castellani, P.J. (2005). *From Snake Pits to Cash Cows; Politics and Public Institutions in New York State*. Albany NY: State University of New York Press.

Cathon, D.E. (2000). The Learning Organization. *Hospital Materiel Management Quarterly*, 21, 3.

Caulier-Grice, J., Mulgan, G. Murray, R. (2010). *The Open Book of Social Innovation* London: NESTA.

Chan, R. (2002). *Guiding Change Journeys, a Synergistic Approach to Organizational-Transformation*. San Francisco CA: Jossey-Bass Publishers.

Chenua-Judge, M. (2001). The Self as an Instrument – A Cornerstone for the Future of OD. *OD Practitioner* 38:3.

Cooperrider, D. L., Whitney, D., & Stavros, J. M. (2003). *Appreciative Inquiry Handbook*. Bedford Heights, OH: Lakeshore Publishers.

Covey, S. (2004). *The 8th Habit: From Effectiveness to Greatness*. New York: Free Press.

Cummings T.G. and Worley C.G. (2005). *Organization Development and Change. 8th ed.* Cincinnati Ohio: South Western Publishers.

Einstein, A and Infeld, L. (1938). *The Evolution of Physics*. Boston MA: Cambridge University Press.

Emery, F.E. and Trist, E.L. (1973). *Toward a Social Ecology*. New York:Plenum.

Follett, M. P. (1924/1951). *Creative Experience*. New York: Peter Smith.

Frankel, V. (2006). *Man's Search for Meaning*. Boston, MA: Beacon Press.

Freidman, E.H. (2007). *A Failure of Nerve, Leadership in the Age of the Quick Fix*. New York: Seabury Books.

Gardner, Howard. (1999). *Intelligence Reframed: Multiple Intelligences for the 21st Century*. New York: Basic Books.

Gold, M. (1980). *Try Another Way Training Manual*. Champaign, Illinois: Research Press.

Goleman, D. (1996). *Emotional Intelligence: Why It Can Matter More Than IQ*. London: Bantam Books.

Hallie, P. (2001). *In the Eye of the Hurricane: Tales of Good and Evil, Help and Harm*. Middleton CT: Wesleyan University.

Heifetz, R. A. and Linsky, M. (2002). *Leadership on the Line, Staying Alive Through the Dangers of Leading*. Boston MA: Harvard School Press.

Heifetz, R.A. and Linsky. (2009). *The Practice of Adaptive Leadership: Tools and Tactics for Changing Your Organization and the World*. Press Boston, MA: Harvard Business.

Hock, D. (1999). *Birth of the Chaordic Age*. San Francisco CA: Berrett-Koecher Publishers.

Individualized Supports Think Tank (2007). Albany, NY: Author. Retrieved from www.sanys. org/ISTTBrochureColorApril92007.pdf.

Kaeufer, K., Scharmer, O.C., and Verteegen, U. (2003). U, Breathing Life into a Dying System: Recreating Health Care from Within. *Reflections* 5:3.

Kendrick., M. (2012). Getting a Good Life: The Challenges for Agency Transformation So That They Are More Person-Centered, *International Journal of Disability, Community and Economic Innovation*. 11:1

Kendrick, M. (2000). Some Initial Thoughts On Establishing Right Relationship Between Staff, Professionals, Service Organizations and the People They Assist. *Queensland Advocacy Incorporated Newsletter* April 2000.

Kolb, D. (1984). *Experiential learning: Experience as the source of learning and development.* Englewood Cliffs, NJ: Prentice-Hall.

Kuhn, T.S. (1996). *The Structure of Scientific Revolutions.* Chicago: University of Chicago Press.

Lewin K. (1943/1997). Defining the Field at a Given Time. In *Resolving Social Conflicts & Field Theory in Social Science*, Washington, D.C.: American Psychological Association.

March, J.G. (2011). A Conversation on Learning About Leadership with Joel Podolin, *Academy of Management Learning & Education*, 10, 3:502–506.

Mary, N.L. (1998) Social Work and the Support Model of Services for People with Developmental Disabilities. *Journal of Social Work Education* 34, 1:.7-15.

Meissner, H. and Mount, B. (2007). *Innovation in Individualized Supports: The NYSACRA Learning Institute.* Albany, NY: New York State Association of Community and Residential Agencies.

Meissner, H. (2011). How the Shift to Individualize Supports Gets Stuck and The First. Step Out of Gridlock. Journal of Intellectual and Developmental Disabilities 49, 5: 383-387.

Mount, B. and Van Eck, S. (2010) *Keys to Life: Creating Customized Homes for People with Disabilities Using Individualized Supports.* Troy, NY:The Arc of Rensselaer County and Capacity Works.

Mount, Beth. (2007). *Lives of Distinction: Creating a Life Path using Individualized Supports.* New York:Job Path.

Morgan, Gareth (1997). *Imaginization: The Art of Creative Management.* Newbury Park CA: Sage Publications.

Nevis, E. (1987). *Organizational Consulting: A Gestalt Approach.* New York: Gardner.

O'Brien, J. (2010). NYSACRA *Learning Institute on Innovation in Individualized Supports A Learning History Phase II: October 2009 – June 2010 Part II – Turning Points.* Albany NY:NYSACRA.

O'Brien, J. and Blessing, C. Editors. (2011). *Conversations on Citizenship and Person-Centered Work.* Toronto: Inclusion Press.

O'Brien, J. and Lyle O'Brien, C. (1988). *A Little Book About Person Centered Planning.* Toronto: Inclusion Press.

O'Reilly, C.A. and Tushman, M.C. (1997). *Winning Through Innovation: A Practical Guide to Leading Organizational Change and Renewal.* Boston MA: Harvard Business School Press.

Owen, H. (2008). *Open Space Technology: A User's Guide.* San Francisco: Berrett-Koehler.

Putnam, R. (2000). *Bowling Alone: The Collapse and Revival of the American Community:* New York: Simon and Schuster.

Raelin, J. (2001). I Don't Have Time to Think versus the Art of Reflective Practice. *Reflections*, 4:1.

Rivera, G. (1972). *Willowbrook: A Report on How It Is and Why It Doesn't Have to Be That Way.* New York: Random House.

Rogers, C. (1961). *On Becoming a Person: A Therapist's View of Psychotherapy.* London: Constable.

Rooke, D. and Torbert B. (2005). Seven Transformations of Leadership. *Harvard Business Review*, 4:1.

Rothman, D. (1971). *The Discovery of the Asylum: Social Order and Disorder in the New Republic.* Boston: Little Brown.

Scharmer, O.C. (2007). *Theory U, Leading From the Future as it Emerges.* Boston:SOL.

Schein, E. (2010). *Organizational Culture and Leadership.* San Francisco CA: Jossey-Bass Publisher.

Schein, E. (1993). On Dialogue, Culture and Organizational Learning. *Organizational Dynamics*, 22.

Senge, P.M., Lichtenstein, B., Kaeufer, K., Bradbury, H. and Carroll, J.S. (2007). Collaborating for Systemic Change. *Sloan Management Review*. Winter.

Senge, P. (2010). *The Fifth Discipline, the Art and Practice of the Learning Organization.* New York, NY: Doubleday Publishers.

Senge, P, Smith B, Schley, S, Laur, and Kruschwitz. (2008). *The Necessary Revolution: How Individuals and Organizations are Working Together to Create a Sustainable World.* New York, NY: Doubleday Publishers.

Torbert, B. (2004). *Action Inquiry, The Secret of Timely and Transforming Leadership.* San Francisco CA: Berrett-Koehler Publishers.

Viesturs, E (with Roberts, D). (2009). *K2, Life and Death on the World's Most Dangerous Mountain.* New York: Broadway Books.

Walker, P. 2011. *"Trusting Our Process:" Organizational Transformation in the Context of a Culture of Innovation – The Arc of Rensselaer County. Organizational Transformation Series* Syracuse NY: The Center on Human Policy.

Weisbord, M.R. and Janoff, S. (1995). *Future Search, An Action Guide to Finding Common Ground in Organizations and Communities.* San Francisco CA: Berrett-Koehler Publishers.

Wheatley, M. (2012). *So Far From Home, lost and found in our brave new world.* San Francisco CA: Berrett-Koehler Publishers.

Wheatley, M (2009). *Turning to One Another: Simple Conversations to Restore Hope to the Future.* San Francisco CA: Berrett-Koehler Publishers.

Wheatley, M. (2001). *Leadership and the New Science. 2nd edition.* San Francisco CA: Berrett-Koehler Publishers.

Zinker, J.C. (1998). *In Search of Good Form: Gestalt Therapy with Couples and Families.* Cleveland, OH: Gestalt Institute of Cleveland Publication.

INCLUSION PRESS
Sample Resources for Your Review

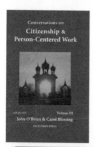

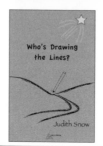

NEW BOOKS

Free Resources:
http://inclusionnetwork.ning.com
(free to view: join to contribute)
See: *The Values of Inclusion* video
and 150 other video clips

Download the Free ipad ibook:
The Values of Inclusion

47 Indian Trail, Toronto,
Ontario Canada M6R 1Z8
p. 416.658.5363   f. 416.658.5067
e. inclusionpress@inclusion.com

Download
our Catalogue:
http://inclusion.com

inclusion.com   BOOKS • WORKSHOPS • MEDIA • RESOURCES